ME AND JIMMY BLUE EYES
GROWING UP WITH THE LAST OF THE GENTLEMAN GANGSTERS

CAROLE CORTLAND RUSSO

Me And Jimmy Blue Eyes

Copyright © 2020 by Carole Cortland Russo

Library of Congress Control Number: 2020913940

ISBN

Paperback 978-1-949864-44-1

Hardcover 978-1-952859-63-2

Digital 978-1-952859-14-4

All rights reserved.

Published by Red Penguin Books

Bellerose Village, New York

No part of this book may be reproduced in any form or by any electronic or mechanical means, including information storage and retrieval systems, without written permission from the author, except for the use of brief quotations in a book review.

To Uncle Jim

This one's for you.

CONTENTS

1. A Stroke—I Wouldn't Recommend It 1
2. Fifty Cents 7
3. Meyer Lansky—A Man Of Principle 15
4. The High Life 27
5. Potatoes Kaufman And The Carpet Joints 41
6. Who Is My Mother? 51
7. Monroe Street 65
8. Bye, Bye, Bugsy 75
9. Uncle Jim Wouldn't Hurt A Fly— 85
10. Havana 93
11. Bad Daughter 103
12. Black Sheep 111
13. Fifty-Fifth Street 121
14. Uncle Jim, Matchmaker 131
15. Ava Sat Here! 141
16. Order Of The Cloom 151
17. Cosa Nostra 157
18. Banjo 165
19. Who Killed George Wood? 175
20. Cooked Up 185
21. Doing Time 197
22. Jimmy And Flo—Like Ham And Eggs 205
23. An Unwelcomed Thought 217
24. Ace In The Hole 227
25. Chewing Gum And Platinum Hair 237
26. The Golden Years 247
27. Blood Of My Blood 259
28. Down But Not Out 267
29. Where's The Money? 279
30. The Home Stretch 287
31. Goodbye To The Old Lion 297
    Epilogue 301

"If"	303
Acknowledgments	305
About the Author	307

Jimmy

A STROKE—I WOULDN'T RECOMMEND IT

Uncle Jim looked up from the morning paper. "Somebody told me the other day that I'm a legend," he said, his eyes wide. "Well, Christ! I don't feel like a legend. I'm just Jimmy."

I leaned against the kitchen sink and observed my uncle, a lovable curmudgeon who, at times, still managed to conjure up the essence of his old machismo. At ninety-five, he was, as he said repeatedly, "… the same old Jimmy."

Even at this advanced age, his face had retained its strength. It was the face of an Indian chief, but I've never heard of an Indian chief whose face could light up with such a smile.

I served him a sticky bun hot from the oven, which filled the house with the aroma of cinnamon. He ate slowly, as was his habit, and I slipped a tape into the machine so that the voice of Alberta Hunter percolated softly, along with the coffee.

Uncle Jim sipped his orange juice. "Who's that?" he asked.

"That's Alberta Hunter."

"Oh, Jesus," he said. "She's an old-timer."

My uncle had attained the ease of *simply being*. The calm you see in dogs and cats and children. Nothing to anticipate. Nothing to fear.

I eat the sticky bun. I read the paper. I have always been here. I will always be here.

That's how it looked to me. I etched this moment in my memory like the Christmas scene in a snow globe.

ON A RED-HOT MORNING IN JULY, Uncle Jim and I boarded a plane and left Florida, headed for New York. He was pissed that he had to be transported through the airport in a wheelchair, but at his age, it was for the best, even though it didn't do anything for his self-image. When we were settled into our seats and the plane took off, his thoughts drifted to his family. He closed his eyes and I listened.

> "My father was a tailor and worked in a factory. He came over here alone. He had two brothers who never followed and I always wondered why he would have left Italy that way. I figured out that he must have been a socialist—maybe had to flee. He used to go to a club every night. It was really just a newspaper and cigar store—but I think it was a meeting place for socialists. They would play cards and drink wine and talk. He fell down a stairwell and died. I think he had too much wine that night."

Uncle Jim laughed and continued, lost in his reminiscences. I was surprised because I had never heard him speak about his father before.

"Now, my brother, Frankie, was a real sucker. He once bought a truckload of hot TVs from his 'Goombah.' Frankie pays him twenty-five hundred dollars and the Goombah tells him the merchandise was stolen out of the warehouse he had it in. So like a schlemiel, Frankie takes the loss. Six months later, it happens again and he comes to me.

"I called the guy up and told him, 'Give my brother back every penny he paid you or I'll cut your goddamned head off, you dirty so-and-so.'"

I looked around at the other seats and gave a nervous smile. If any of the other passengers could hear Uncle Jim's gravelly voice, they were getting an earful.

When we arrived at LaGuardia, Uncle Jim's nephew, his brother's son, Frankie Jr., was waiting to drive us into Manhattan. We got to the Fifty-Fifth Street apartment, and the three of us passed through the familiar bustle of activity on the sidewalk into the cool darkness of the lobby, where we were cheerfully greeted by Raphael, the long-time doorman. On the ninth floor, Uncle Jim fumbled a little with the keys before he was able to unlock the door. Inside, he carefully lowered his frail body onto the tattered white sofa, and there he sat, breathing in the past, as light streamed through the tall windows, illuminating the air so that particles of dust danced around his silver hair.

It had been ten years since my aunt passed away and, even before her death, the apartment had been going downhill. As Uncle Jim sat quietly among his wife's things: the silver, the porcelain, the fine English furniture—once cherished and pampered, now dusty and neglected—he seemed to be absorbing the atmosphere as if he took nourishment from it.

"I grew old in this apartment," he said.

I had the realization that this would be the last time he would come here. Gently, we explained to him that it was unwise for him to stay by himself in the city.

"You better come out to my house, Unca Jimmy," Frankie stammered. He was a nervous type. Thin, with a forgettable face and bad teeth.

It wasn't easy telling Uncle Jim what to do. But he reluctantly agreed to go with Frankie to Long Island. He looked weary and when he said, "All right, I'll go," it was with a kind of resignation I'd not seen before.

His bony chest rose and fell as he heaved a sigh. "I'm on my way out," he said. "Don't you think I know that?"

It was killing me to see my uncle declining by inches, like an old lion losing a little more ground every day. Downstairs, he shook Raphael's hand solemnly, and bid him a final goodbye. Then he drove off in Frankie's car and I went back upstairs.

For the rest of the day and on into the evening, I cleaned. I don't know why. I polished some silver, dusted the perfume bottles. These objects had my aunt's DNA on them. As long as the place was filled with them, she was still there. Address books, buttons, rosary beads, photos. She held on to so many things. I found old linens dry-cleaned and folded neatly in a chest along with a sequined jumpsuit from some time the Forties. Why did she save that? Old cards, bits of paper, expired medicines. I don't want to come here anymore! Coming here is like being in a graveyard.

That night, I got undressed and placed my clothes on a small chair in the master bedroom. Under the chair, I placed my sneakers and socks. I turned on the light in the guest bathroom to act as a night light, and went to bed, thinking of my uncle and saddened by all the loss and letting go.

The next morning, when I woke up, I noticed the light in the guest bathroom was *off*. When I went in to investigate, I found my socks hanging neatly on the towel rack. I knew I didn't put them there. I didn't turn the light off.

I got dressed, gathered up my things, and got the hell out of there as fast as I possibly could.

I, too, went to Long Island, where I spent a few days over the Fourth of July weekend with friends. The plan was for Uncle Jim and me to fly back to Florida together.

At the airport, Frankie delivered my uncle to me in a pitiful state. His eyes were puffed and half closed, his skin was gray, and he was slumped in a wheelchair, barely conscious I was shocked at his condition.

"What happened?" I asked.

Providing no explanation, a visibly nervous Frankie, with tears in his eyes, quickly scurried off into the crowd, leaving me to board the plane with my fragile cargo. As the flight attendants lifted my uncle into his seat, I warned them to be prepared for a death during the flight. This was my fear.

We lifted off, leaving behind us the Bronx, where the boy, Jimmy, once fought on a hill, Long Island, where Jimmy once stood at the water's edge, receiving whiskey from the boats that delivered it, and Manhattan, where he'd created a life born of his ambition, and to where I knew he would never return.

He languished beside me, his face a death mask. I looked to see if he was still breathing and when his hands jerked spasmodically, I knew he was still alive. Delirious, he struggled to stand, to get out.

"No, Uncle Jim. You have to stay put. We're going home."

His hands moved like spiders, aimlessly, over the blanket across his legs. His eyes seemed stitched shut. I held my breath, praying that he would make it off this plane alive.

We landed in Fort Lauderdale, where my uncle was loaded into a wheelchair and whisked out of the plane. Once inside the terminal, I called 911. My husband Joe, who was scheduled to meet us, arrived along with the ambulance, and we rushed to the hospital where I was told that my uncle's brain was bleeding and he most probably wouldn't survive.

Seated next to my uncle in intensive care, I looked around at the cubicle with its white cabinets and tabletops covered with medical supplies. Uncle Jim lay on a high gurney, covered by a sheet. His body seemed tiny, his face—the face of an Indian chief—in repose.

I suddenly remembered that Frankie Jr. had managed to shove a wad of money into Uncle Jim's pocket before he left us—saying it was cash that the old man had brought with him from Florida. I looked around until I spotted his clothing lying in a rumpled heap on a chair in the corner of the cubicle. I picked up his gray trousers, reached into the pocket, and, much to my relief, the bankroll had not been lost or stolen in all the confusion. *Leave it to you, Uncle Jim.* My uncle, hanging on to life by a thread, had been traveling with ten thousand dollars in his pocket.

The irony of it wasn't lost on me as I recollected Uncle Jim's humble beginnings.

FIFTY CENTS

My uncle, Vincent Alo, was widely known from the Thirties through the full span of the twentieth century as "Jimmy Blue Eyes." Mobster. In his earlier years, Uncle Jim was tight-lipped, a necessity for the life he lived, but as he approached his nineties, he began to talk. Once he got started, he became quite a storyteller. And I was all ears. Over the course of a decade, during countless restaurant conversations, I listened as my uncle revisited his past.

> My old man was a nice guy. I only saw him angry once. Some friends and I were playin' craps on the street. A neighborhood cop took us down to the station just to scare us. My father came to get me. He said I had disgraced the family—and kicked me right in the ass. He was never around too much. But I remember one time when I was four or five years old. We lived a few blocks from the East River and I fell into the water. There were always a lotta bums hangin' around over by the pier and one of them jumped in and saved me. My father gave him fifty cents. I guess that's what he thought I was worth.

To me, this was a metaphor for my uncle's life—and everything that came after was his way to prove his father wrong.

JIMMY'S FATHER, Salvatore Alo, came to America from Calabria, Italy, in 1884 at the age of eighteen. He was a tailor by trade and found work in a garment factory. After years of loneliness, he was able to arrange a marriage and his stranger/bride, eighteen-year-old Julia Scalzo, arrived in New York from Calabria in 1901. Their firstborn came at home on May 26, 1904, in East Harlem, which, in those days, was an Italian neighborhood. His parents had him christened Vincent, but he would always be called Jimmy. His sister, Elizabeth, was born two years later and two brothers, Frank and Joseph followed.

Young Jimmy

Julia Alo was a taskmaster and stood for no nonsense from her brood. She saw to it that her children went to church on Sunday and said their prayers every night. Her heavy-handed treatment sparked a rebellious spirit in Jimmy. But in spite of it, he dreamed of making something of himself. He was a choirboy, sold newspapers, and shined shoes. A bit shy, he tended to stutter when nervous; but that never held him back. He was fun loving and full of energy. Though small and wiry, he packed a surprising wallop and was always game for a fight. He broke his left arm so often doctors threatened him with amputation. At thirteen, after a final break, he was hospitalized for a bone graft, one of the earliest ever performed. His teacher, Mrs. Gottleman, came to visit him in the hospital. For the rest of his life he would recall her kindness.

> She was a cripple. I'll never forget. She brought me books to read. The Horatio Alger stories. And the Richard Carvel books about how an English boy overcame hardships and made good. But the best was the poem, *IF* by Rudyard Kipling. She brought me that poem and I've tried to live by it. I've never forgotten the way she made it her business to come and see me like that. It made quite an impression on me.

1918. Woodrow Wilson was in the White House. The Armistice was signed in Europe. The Great War was over and soon Johnny would come marching home. It was a good year for the country and a good year for young Jimmy. It pleased his mother to see him graduate from public school, having completed grade nine. Several months later, with the help of a family friend, he landed a job as an apprentice at a prominent financial house, Haydon, Stone, and Company. He was fourteen.

Jimmy on street

Every morning, Jimmy would leave his Bronx neighborhood, hop the train, and ride into Manhattan. Perched on a wicker seat, he gazed through the dusty windows and watched the squat buildings of Jerome Avenue morph into the skyscrapers of the city. He must have envisioned his destiny, since arriving each day at his Wall Street job, he entered another world—one that held promise for a young man from humble beginnings in the Italian ghetto. He was smarter than most—he knew that. He had curiosity and couldn't get enough of reading books, especially about great men of history.

Much of his spare time was spent playing basketball, baseball, and boxing. He was popular with both boys and girls—a good dancer, too. On weekends, there were ball games, dances, and picnics with beer and sandwiches. He wore knickers and caps and shoes that laced up the ankles. His skin was a pale olive, his hair dark. He had a high, domed forehead and his brown eyes were smallish, but clear and intense. His nose had already lost its shape—a result of many punches. Still, his face was pleasing—some would even say handsome—especially when he flashed his thousand-watt smile.

At home, his mother, the shrike from whom his timid sister, Lizzie, would never break away, kept the railroad flat clean enough to eat off the floor. The toilet was communal, shared with three other families. Baths were once a week in a large tub in the kitchen and no one wanted to be the last one in. There was always enough to eat and the smell of garlic browning in olive oil made home seem inviting. If affection was not to be forthcoming from mother or father, at least the siblings were there for each other.

Years later, during one of our dinner conversations, Uncle Jim revealed his resentment towards his mother.

> I always felt that my mother ruined my sister's life, forcing her into an arranged marriage with a loud-mouthed Italian who came over from Calabria. I think she was preparing me for the same thing—but she had the wrong boy. My brother, Frankie, went into the bookmaking business and made a lotta money. He told her he had a job. I think he wanted to follow in my footsteps, but my mother didn't want that. She wanted him to be a tailor like our father. Anyway, he'd bought some expensive suits and when she found out what he was doin' she took a pair of shears and cut them up. Oh, she was a strong woman.

In the Bronx, life was lived mainly on the streets, which teemed with pushcarts, peddlers, candy stores, green grocers and butcher shops with sawdust on the floor and live chickens in cages. It was around this time that Jimmy acquired the nickname that would stay with him for the rest of his life.

It's a funny story. I'm about fourteen years old. In those days, they held dances every Sunday night after the basketball games. Well, I was very active and I boxed. So I go to a dance this one Sunday night. And the day before, I'd been boxin' at the gym and the other guy landed a pretty good one and I had a black and blue eye—which wasn't unusual because I was known for gettin' into scrapes. Anyway, I'm at this dance and my cousins were there—six girls. So the girls are on one side of the room and the boys on the other and the band starts playin' a song that was popular at the time, "Why Are Your Brown Eyes Blue." Somethin' like that. And I had these black and blue eyes and all, and my cousins start chantin', "Come on, Blue Eyes. Come on and dance!" And the name stuck.

JIMMY WAS LIVING in two separate worlds. Both the upper crust of Wall Street and the poor, tough streets of the neighborhood. Sometimes he hung out in pool halls or played craps with friends. Around him, there were plenty of antidotes to poverty. Theft, gambling, loan-sharking, strong-arming, and prostitution. Lawlessness was everywhere, but Jimmy held himself above it, counting on dreams and ambition to keep him on a steady course.

By the spring of 1923, he was becoming restless. Working hard at his job, he had earned the title of Broker Apprentice, but others who were hired after him moved up while he was passed over for promotion. He decided to speak up. Standing in front of his supervisor's desk, he broached the subject. He was polite and stated his case, but the answer he got hit him hard.

"Alo," his boss said, "you just mind your business and let me tend to mine."

There were no Italians working on Wall Street in those days. The guys who were bein' promoted were mostly English or German. I didn't realize it then, that I was bein' discriminated against. I told my boss, "Screw you!" and I quit. I never looked for another job.

Now, he was adrift and needed money. His mother thought he should take up tailoring like his father, even open up a haberdashery someday. Jimmy scoffed at that idea. It wasn't for him to be stuck in a sweatshop, earning a meager living. No more was he going to knuckle under some abusive boss. Not when there were men out in the neighborhood who were spiffy dressers and carried wads of money in their pockets. People respected them. They carried with them a tradition from the old country that came across the ocean along with the rags and mementos—that certain *something* in the nature of Italians that thumbed its nose at authority and took care of its own problems. Jimmy was one of them and he knew it. From where he stood, there weren't many options available. He had tried the straight and narrow. That didn't work. So what would be *his* antidote to poverty? He found it on the streets of his neighborhood. Jimmy and three companions attempted to stick up a jewelry store at gunpoint. Jimmy was apprehended while the others fled.

"I had the jewelry and I got caught holding the bag," he told me. "Those Irish cops would beat the hell out of you back then. They got me good. I did a bad thing and I did time."

At nineteen, Jimmy was sentenced to prison for five to twelve years on the charge of armed robbery. Refusing to name his cohorts, he was taken to Sing Sing, where he was processed and transferred to Dannemora in the Adirondacks, which was known as the Siberia of New York. He spent weeks at a time in the "cooler," the prison term for the lightless, frigid isolation cells below ground, where brutish guards wielding clubs administered frequent beatings. He received no mail from his mother who would never completely forgive him for "disgracing the family."

On August 16, 1927, a transformed and toughened man of twenty-four walked out of prison to resume his life. He was still the same Jimmy, but his character and resolve, forged by the cruelty of the past five years, had hardened into stone.

MEYER LANSKY—A MAN OF PRINCIPLE

1929. It was a watershed year—the year of the great crash. The Roaring Twenties were drawing to a close and the Great Depression was just around the corner. Hoover was in the White House and Mrs. Hoover shocked the nation by having *a colored lady*, opera singer Marion Anderson, to tea. Jimmy Walker was still mayor of New York. Primo Carnera, the giant from Italy, was being touted as the new heavyweight boxing sensation. Damon Runyun's Broadway fables blended show business and the underworld and Walter Winchell, writing for the *New York Mirror*, borrowed the phrase "making whoopee" from Rudyard Kipling and made it popular. Texas Guinan was greeting New York cafe patrons by shouting, "Hello, Suckers!" and they loved it. In Hollywood, the glamorization of the gangster had already begun.

Prohibition had spawned a new industry—bootlegging. An unprecedented wave of crime and violence was erupting in cities across the country. Chicago harbored the toughest of the tough. Ever since gang leader Dion O'Banion was shot to death in his flower shop, a blood feud existed between his friend George "Bugs" Moran and the notorious "Scarface" Al Capone.

On Valentine's Day, three men walked into a garage at 2122 Clark Street in Chicago, lined up seven men against the wall, and executed them. The only living thing left behind was Highball, a German shepherd belonging to one of the victims. The dog's howls alerted neighbors who discovered the horror.

In New York, Arnold Rothstein headed a cast of characters who would become crime legends. Rothstein, the son of Jewish immigrants, had an uncanny ability to figure odds, which enabled him to win at any type of gambling he undertook. He is best remembered for bribing eight players on the Chicago White Sox baseball team to throw the World Series in 1919. In bootlegging, he shared the turf with Waxey Gordon, Owney Madden, and Dutch Schultz.

Schultz, whose real name was Arthur Flegenheimer, grew up in the Bronx. He went on to form a gang of some of the toughest criminals of the day. Known as the Beer Baron of the Bronx, he had managed to eliminate rivals "Legs" Diamond and Vincent "Mad Dog" Coll, by 1932.

Jimmy Blue Eyes was playing on this court. Together with his partner, Bart Salvo, Jimmy would drive past the potato fields to the eastern end of Long Island and meet the ships that carried whiskey down from Canada. The booze would be loaded onto cars or trucks and transported back to Manhattan and the Bronx. They carried guns in case they ran into hijackers, and cash in case they ran into the law. Life was good and Jimmy was making money.

While in Dannemora, Jimmy struck up a friendship with two brothers, Johnny and Jimmy McCabe, who were serving time for bank robbery. When the brothers were released from prison, they resumed their profession. The question as to whether or not

Jimmy became their partner in the bank business is anybody's guess.

In the summer of 1928, Johnny McCabe was arrested again. One morning, Uncle Jimmy visited his friend in the Bronx County Jail. Later that day, brandishing a pair of handguns, Johnny McCabe attempted to break out. He killed two guards before committing suicide by turning a gun on himself. The police sought Vincent "Jimmy Blue Eyes" Alo as the accomplice who had visited the jail that day and somehow managed to pass the guns to McCabe.

Jimmy was on the lam and he had to keep a low profile. He adopted the alias "Casale" and lived like an outlaw in drab furnished rooms in New Jersey or on Long Island. Anywhere, as long as it was off the beaten track.

One night, half a century later, during dinner at Patsy's Restaurant, Uncle Jim took a long sip of wine, set the glass down and spoke about McCabe with emotion.

> A friend of mine was in jail and I tried to bust him out. I must have been crazy to do it. But he was a good friend, a very sweet guy—and I knew he would've done it for me. In those days if you were a four-time loser, you faced life. He couldn't handle that. He killed himself and took two guards with him.

1929 WAS a primary year in Jimmy's life. In that year he would meet Florence Miller aka Flo Hart, the woman who would become his wife—and Meyer Lansky, the man with whom he would be most closely associated throughout his life. Uncle Jim explained to me how he met Meyer.

Flo

I had a friend, Mike Lascari. He was in the beer business. Some guys I knew wanted to kill him and take over his business. I didn't think that was right so I got ahold of him and told him to lay low for a while. His partner at the time was Charlie FLucky (Luciano). Mike appreciated me lettin' him know what was goin' on and he asked me to meet with Charlie about this. When we met, he had this little guy with him. That was Meyer Lansky. I had never heard of him. But we were immediately attracted to one another. He was a man of principle. We could talk about a lot of things. I can't think of anyone that I admire more than Meyer. He really educated me.

MEYER LANSKY WAS BORN Meyer Suchowljansky in 1902, in Grodno, which at that time was part of the Russian Empire under Czar Nicholas II. When he was ten, his family fled to America to escape the brutal form of anti-Semitism that the Jews of his region were facing. The family settled in Brownsville, a tough area of Brooklyn—relocating several years later to Manhattan's Lower East Side. They adopted the surname "Lansky" which was easier to pronounce in America than Suchowljansky.

Meyer and his younger brother, Jake, attended school together, where Meyer proved to be an exemplary student. At thirteen, he was Bar Mitzvah and seemed to be an ideal son, both studious and respectful. The sidewalks, however, offered a counterpoint to the traditional life in the Lansky household. On Delancey Street or Houston or Grand, a boy like Meyer with his talent for figures could excel at the game of craps and come home with plenty of money to hide under the mattress.

Toughness was required and little Meyer, no more than five feet five, had that going for him. It was on these streets that he first encountered Benjamin Siegel, who would become one of his closest friends. Siegel was a few years younger than Meyer. Good-looking, with a wild, flamboyant personality, he soon learned to look up to his newly acquired pal who was, by contrast, brainy and introverted.

In the years between 1914 and 1920, Meyer was working in a machine shop as an apprentice tool-and-die maker. He racked up several arrests for minor infractions and, with the advent of Prohibition, abandoned his job as a machinist, never to be "employed" again.

Like Jimmy, Meyer formed early friendships that would span a lifetime. First and foremost was his relationship with his brother, Jake, who would always be by his side. But the men who came out of the ghetto with him would prove to be almost as close. Red Levine, Doc Stacher, Ben "Bugsy" Siegel. These were the tough Jews who came up with him.

One evening, as Meyer walked home alone, he was surrounded by a gang of young Italians who demanded money in exchange for not beating the hell out of him. Replying, "Go fuck yourselves!" he earned the instant respect of the gang leader, one Charlie Luciano. This street tough was known as "Lucky" due to his good fortune at cards and craps. An instant rapport grew between the Italian and the Jew that would eventually lead to the development of a crime syndicate that would capture the attention of the country.

1929 WAS ALSO a year of transition for Jimmy Blue Eyes. He had already come in contact with most of the major players. He knew Owney Madden and Waxey Gordon. Handsome Joe Adonis from Brooklyn was a close pal. Jimmy and his partner, Bart, brought the whiskey in from Long Island and distributed it to speakeasies in the Bronx, Westchester, and Manhattan. They didn't bother anybody else's territory and they made sure nobody bothered theirs.

Jimmy was twenty-four, attractive, and beginning a lifelong habit of paying meticulous attention to his grooming and wardrobe. Despite his status as a lamster, he was moving freely around the city. Manhattan was a small town and Jimmy was making it his own. There was a restaurant on every corner and the speakeasies and cabarets were filled with music, laughter and camaraderie. The Great White Way offered entertainment such as *George White's Scandals* and the *Ziegfeld Follies*, with their plethora of gorgeous girls.

One of the Broadway hangouts was the drugstore in the Piccadilly Hotel. In the heart of the theater district on 45th Street, next to the Music Box Theater, the Piccadilly was a central spot for show business and the underworld to converge. Among the people who hung out there was a Broadway character known as Banjo. His real name was Benjamin Contrada and he lived at the Piccadilly Hotel. He was a small-time operator who made his living bankrolling crap games. A scuffler, content to make his nut and keep life simple, he wasn't a tough guy but he knew how to navigate the territory.

One summer afternoon, Banjo was having a sandwich in the Piccadilly Drugstore when in walked Flo Hart. Flo was a pony, which is a showgirl who can dance a little and is too short to be one of those statuesque beauties parading around in skimpy costumes and towering headpieces. Banjo, whose idea of a good time was taking twelve chorus girls out for a spaghetti dinner, never learned to drive. He had a car and driver waiting outside, and he asked Flo if she'd like to take a ride in the cool of his automobile. Flo said, "Why not?" and off they went.

Jimmy Blue Eyes waited outside a cigar store, shaded by a red and green striped awning that jutted out over the sidewalk. He watched the black sedan glide up to the curb. Banjo got out and walked over to where Jimmy was leaning against an iron banister, switching a toothpick from one side of his mouth to the other. As they concluded their business, Jimmy glanced over at the car and spotted a shapely pair of legs.

"Who's the dame in the car?" Jimmy asked.

"I know her from around town. She's a hoofer—a nice kid."

"Mind if I go over and say 'hello?'"

"Naw. Be my guest," Banjo answered.

Jimmy sauntered over to the car and leaned down. He tipped his straw hat and found himself looking into a striking face.

"Well…what are *you* lookin' at?" She challenged him, her alabaster face encircled by coal black hair.

He looked into her eyes, which were the color of root beer, and waited. She broke into a smile. Since he was on the lam, he introduced himself as Jimmy Casale—and asked for a date.

Even though she had a boyfriend at the time, she said, "I guess that would be okay."

They went out together that night. She ordered eggs because she didn't know if he had much money. They chatted about people they knew and the name of Jimmy Blue Eyes came up.

"I never met him," she said. "And I don't want to. I hear he's a terrible person."

Within a few weeks, Jimmy managed to clear up the issue of his true identity and successfully defend his character. The boyfriend became a thing of the past and Jimmy and Flo moved in together. They didn't have a lot of money but they found they could live on love. She washed the sheets in the bathtub of their Long Island flat. She had one good black dress and a really spiffy pair of two-toned spectator pumps. They couldn't get married right away since she hadn't as yet bothered to divorce William Miller, the man she had married at fifteen.

It didn't matter to Jimmy when Flo told him that she had two little boys who lived in Seaford on the southern shore of Long Island, with their grandmother. Jimmy was all for family. Besides, the boys weren't going to be living with "Mr. and Mrs. Casale."

Jimmy didn't own a car but his partner, Bart, did. Since it was summer, they spent their days on the beach with friends or rowing on a lake or picnicking. Flo proved to be congenial and wisecracking and an all-around good egg. She fit in easily with Jimmy's circle and developed a strong friendship with Bart's redheaded wife, Tex. It was a happy-go-lucky time and they were young and in love.

One night, not long after they became a couple, Flo was startled by banging on the door of their flat. When she opened it, there was Jimmy, held up by Bart. Beneath his jacket, his torso was wrapped in bloodstained bandages.

"What happened?" she sputtered, as they lowered him onto the living room couch.

"A friend shot me by accident."

"Did you go to a hospital?"

"Hospital!" he said, his eyes widening. "Nah. They brought me to a doctor we know. He patched me up."

It may have been at that moment the full magnitude of what she had gotten herself into began to come into focus. She was going to have to cultivate a stiff upper lip—and she would prove equal to the task.

In later years, Uncle Jim never tired of telling his favorite story about Flo.

> I used to be in charge of pickin' up the whiskey when the boats came in on Long Island. We'd be out there in the marshes with speedboats and the whiskey would come in from Canada and England. Long Island was a wilderness in those days and we'd be out there till all hours of the night. So this one night when I finally got home, it's pretty late and I say to Flo,
>
> "What's for dinner?"
>
> "There's no dinner," she says.

"Why is that?" I says.

"I gave it to the dog."

"Why did you do that?"

"You were late so I gave your dinner to the dog," she says. "Why didn't you call?"

I says, "There wasn't a phone booth for a hundred miles!"

"Well, I gave your dinner to the dog and what's more, I'm never cookin' for you again."

"Well, that's okay with me," I says, "'Cause I never liked your cookin' anyhow."

She had something in her hand and she threw it at me. And ya know, from then on we just ate out every night. But that was okay. Because New York had the best restaurants in the world.

ME AND JIMMY BLUE EYES

Hawaii 1934

THE HIGH LIFE

November 1932. FDR defeated Herbert Hoover in a landslide victory. The country mourned the death of the Lindberg baby. Actor Paul Muni's portrayal of Al Capone in the movie *Scarface* elevated him to stardom. And while Edward G. Robinson in *Little Caesar* was everybody's idea of a gangster, Jimmy Blue Eyes was the real McCoy.

People all over the country were standing in line for hours to get an apple or a loaf of bread, but Prohibition had provided Jimmy and his pals with the proverbial pot of gold.

My uncle spoke more and more about the events of his life. At times his candor startled me.

> Arnold Rothchild bankrolled a lot of the bootleggin' that went on in New York. Dutch Schultz, now he was a very mean guy. He was in the bootleggin' and numbers business. We were all in the beer business. In those days, the breweries were makin' near beer after the Volstead Act was passed and a lot of the breweries had been shut down. Owney Madden and his partners took charge of some

of those breweries, paid off the law. They were makin' beer. Pretty good beer. Then we'd distribute the beer to saloons and speakeasies. Our area was up in Westchester.

During the first few years of the 1930s, Jimmy's friendship with Meyer deepened. They were alike in many ways. Avid readers, interested in history and current affairs. Both of them were low-key and soft-spoken. They both possessed "common sense," a quality that Mark Twain said was "not very common,"—a quote that Jimmy enjoyed repeating. They must have also shared an ability to be ruthless when necessary, even though, within the framework of their world, they both insisted upon honor as they understood it.

The unintended consequence of the Volstead Act, which was a misguided attempt to legislate morality, was that previously law-abiding citizens became willing to disobey the law.

Cynicism, hypocrisy, and disrespect for authority spread like an airborne illness. Unpopular and impossible to implement, the 18th Amendment was repealed two years into FDR's presidency.

"The boys" had to find other ways to make a buck and gambling was a natural—something that had always been part of the street life. Jimmy and his partners turned to the numbers business in their old territory, the Bronx and Westchester.

Jimmy, Flo, and Prohibition Partner Tommy Milo in Havana

"The numbers business wasn't easy, but we did it," Uncle Jim told me. "A fella needed to be bankrolled and we were the only ones with any money. We made so much money, we didn't know what to do with it."

KIDNAPPING WAS common practice in those days—in those circles. In 1934, Jimmy's partner, Bart Salvo, was snatched. When Uncle Jim told me about this, he related it as if he were talking about what he had for breakfast.

Bart was kidnapped by a little rag-tag gang of three. The ransom money was paid and Bart was returned unharmed. The police interrogated him; but, true to the code of the underworld, he refused to say who his kidnappers were. As a result, he did a couple of years in Dannemora for Obstruction of Justice. One of the kidnappers ratted on the other two and all three wound up in Dannemora. In other words, Bart found himself in jail with his abductors. After a couple of years, Charlie Lucky told Jimmy that the three kidnappers had a chance for a new trial and Jimmy should see to it that they got a good lawyer. It was taken care of and they got off with time served. According to Jimmy, this was an example of the kind of guy Charlie Lucky was. He felt they had served time and that was enough. End of story.

Well, not quite. Within a few years after they were released from prison—all three of the fellows who snatched Bart wound up dead.

WHILE JIMMY WAS MAKING a living with the numbers, Meyer focused his attention on Saratoga Springs in upstate New York. Located in the foothills of the Adirondacks, Saratoga was an elegant summer resort. It had horse racing, therapeutic baths, charming Victorian hotels, fine dining, and casinos. Although gambling was illegal, the local authorities had been looking the other way for decades. Arnold Rothstein had operated in Saratoga since the twenties and now Meyer went into action there—taking over the most successful of the Saratoga casinos, The Piping Rock. His principle partners were Frank Costello, who owned the Copacabana in Manhattan and Joseph Doto aka Joe Adonis.

These were transitional years for Jimmy and Meyer. They had both succeeded in propelling themselves out of poverty. They had survived Prohibition. They had become family men. They wanted to put behind them the memory of any rash acts that may have characterized their youth. They craved respectability and hoped money could buy it.

In 1930, Meyer's wife, Anne, gave birth to a child. They named him Bernard, but he would always be called Buddy. By the middle of his second year, the baby was diagnosed with cerebral palsy. His mother became convinced that Buddy's affliction was the direct result of the sins of his father. It was "God's retribution," she said. Anne passed her convictions on to Meyer, constantly berating him.

There was an incident that has been written about time and time again. As the story goes, Meyer broke down under the stress of his wife's hysterical harangues. He and Jimmy traveled to Boston, where they rented a hotel room. The normally abstinent Meyer went on a binge that lasted for a week. Jimmy stayed with his friend as he cried and drank. Finally, Meyer pulled himself together. After that, they drove back to Manhattan and it was never mentioned again.

Meyer and Anne moved into the Majestic, a luxury apartment building on Seventy-Seventh Street and Central Park West (where they occasionally shared the elevator with columnist and neighbor, Walter Winchell). Ben and Esther Siegel lived at the Waldorf Astoria for a time, as did Charlie Lucky. Jimmy and Flo had an apartment on Seventy-Second Street, at 22 Riverside Drive.

Flo, Meyer and Anne Lansky at the beach

All three women were customers at Wilma's, an exclusive dress shop on Fifty-Seventh Street. They spent hours seated in comfortable chairs, sipping coffee, and gossiping, while their favorite sales ladies brought them things to try on. The proper wardrobe was essential in the quest for class and upward mobility and being waited on like royalty brought with it a delicious sense of exclusivity that blotted out any unpleasant feelings of unworthiness.

Flo yearned for the finer things. She had to have a piano and it had to be a Steinway Baby Grand. But while she appreciated elegance, at the same time, she had an appealing down-to-earth quality.

She hired a piano teacher who came to the apartment twice a week, where she always met him wearing a housedress and bedroom slippers. No make-up, no hairdo. One evening, Flo and Anne, wanting to soak up some culture, attended a concert at

Carnegie Hall. As they descended a sweeping staircase, Flo, gloriously coifed and gowned, spotted the piano teacher. She went over to say "Hello," and he stared blankly at her, trying to figure out who she was. She and Anna thought that was hilarious.

FOR JIMMY AND FLO, every night was a night out. The best spots were Dinty Moore's for homestyle cooking, the Villanova for Italian food, and the former speakeasy, Frankie & Johnny's for the best steaks and chops. Leon & Eddy's on Fifty-Second, was a favorite cabaret. They also hit Connie's Inn in Harlem and the Cotton Club, which was owned by friend, Owney Madden.

Flo's job was to look beautiful and keep an elegant home; and she lived up to it. With her competitive nature, she was driven to have the best and be the best. She and Jimmy made a dazzling couple. They were photographed night after night, smiling as they dined and clubbed with friends in Manhattan, Saratoga, Havana—wherever there was fun to be had. It was said of them that Jimmy and Flo went together like ham and eggs. But although he enjoyed his wife's company—there is no doubt that Jimmy was happiest in the company of his male friends. He loved them—and they loved him in return.

One place that Jimmy went without Flo was Hot Springs, Arkansas. That was a trip he usually made a couple of times a year with his cronies. There's a snapshot of him sitting astride a horse, outfitted in equestrian finery. He wears riding boots and carries a riding crop. In another, taken on the same day, he is seated on the steps of the Arlington Hotel. Four men surround him, and one of them has his arms draped casually around Jimmy's shoulders. Lounging on the steps, above the group, is Ben Siegel, wearing a cap and smoking a cigar.

Hot Springs. Boys on the steps.

There was always a lot of good-natured kibitzing that went on between Jimmy and his pals—like the time when he and Ben were visiting Hot Springs together. Unbeknownst to Ben, Jimmy borrowed his clubs to play a round of golf. After making a bad shot, Jimmy, who took the game seriously, lost his temper and broke the golf club on a tree.

"Jesus, Jimmy, we'd better tell them back at the clubhouse that you broke Ben's stick," says one of *the boys*.

"Like hell we will," says Jimmy.

They go back to the clubhouse to shower and change clothes. Suddenly, Ben walks in, goes directly to his clubs, and counts them. "Hey, one of my clubs is missing," he yells. "Some bastard must have stolen it!"

They all burst out laughing, including Jimmy. Naturally, somebody had tipped Ben off, providing him an opportunity to give Jimmy a good ribbing.

There was plenty of laughter and somebody was always cooking up a practical joke. Meyer's sense of humor tended more toward dry observation, which Uncle Jim never failed to appreciate.

> Flo and I were having dinner, along with Meyer and Anne, at Ben and Esther Siegel's house on Long Island. Esther was a little pretentious and was dyin' to belong to Jewish "society." During dinner, she let it be known that she was studying French. Well, Meyer thought for a minute and then he said, in that quiet voice of his, "Don't you think you should learn English first?"

JIMMY AND FLO were living a fairytale existence. In the morning, when they opened their eyes, the first thing they saw was a carved gilt mirror that hung above a green marble chest-of-drawers that stood opposite the bed. Jimmy would pull on his silk robe, slide his small, well-shaped feet into bedroom slippers and pad quietly into the kitchen, where Flo puttered around, her long lacquered fingernails inadequate for producing anything more than the simplest breakfast. Toast and coffee. Grapefruit and a poached egg.

After breakfast, he would dress, handling his clothes carefully. He wore the finest trousers, jackets, and handmade shoes. His overcoats were smartly cut. He made it a point never to wear black. After kissing Flo goodbye, he would hop a cab to the Waldorf Astoria barbershop for a shave.

The barbershop was a daily ritual. The large, comfortable chairs trimmed with chrome and softened by deep red leather perched high above the black and white tiled floor. From the chair hung a black leather strap on which the barbers sharpened their instruments. Shoeshine 'boys' stood by, wearing their brown, congenial faces, in the event that the gentlemen's shoes needed attention while they relaxed with their heads swathed in hot towels.

Later, in the afternoon and evening, Jimmy would take care of any business that needed to be transacted. For the most part, it went smoothly for him. The fearsome reputation he had earned during his twenties had become as good as gold. A man would have to think twice before crossing him.

When Fiorella LaGuardia was swept into office as the mayor of New York, he declared war on corruption and made his intentions known by having a large number of slot machines rounded up and loaded onto a barge where he proceeded to smash them into pieces with a sledgehammer and toss them into Long Island Sound. He appointed Thomas E. Dewey as the city's Special Prosecutor and Dewey was determined to break the back of the rackets in New York. It wasn't long before he focused his attention on the notorious Dutch Schultz.

By the early Thirties, Jimmy was part of a crime *syndicate*—a sort of commission—that had been formed with Lucky Luciano, Meyer Lansky, and Frank Costello at the helm. These men, who had the knack of leadership, were attempting to make decisions and enforce rules that would benefit the majority, maximize their ability to function successfully, and keep some control over the general goings-on.

There had always been a division between the younger Italians and the older "Mustachio Petes" who came to America as adults at the turn of the century. The more Americanized wise guys had little patience for their older counterparts, such as Salvatore Maranzano and Joe "The Boss" Masseria. The young hoods weren't interested in restricting their activities to include only Italians. By and by, Maranzano and Masseria were eliminated.

It was understood that unbridled murderous behavior only created *heat* for everybody. Dutch Schultz was a case in point. Infuriated by the Special Prosecutor's interference with his livelihood, Schultz made widely known his intention to murder Dewey. The commission could not ignore this witless move.

On the evening of October 23, 1935, Schultz, his accountant, Otto "Abbadabba" Berman and two of his henchman, Abe Landau and Lulu Rosenkrantz, were having dinner at the Palace Chop House in Newark, New Jersey. The Dutchman had gone to the washroom when a man entered and walked to the rear of the restaurant. Opening the door of the men's room, he found Schultz there and shot him twice. As he fled, he passed the table where Berman, Landau, and Rosenkrantz were seated, shooting them, as well. Mortally wounded, the four men were taken to the Newark City Hospital.

While Dutch Schultz lingered, Police Sergeant Luke Conlon tried to extract from him the identity of his executioners. This, he could not do. Occasionally interrupted by Sergeant Conlon's fruitless attempts at interrogation, the Dutchman, out of his head, raved on for hours. Here's some of what he had to say:

"George, don't make no full moves. Oh, Mama, Mama, Mama. Oh, oh, dog biscuits—and when he is happy he doesn't get snappy. The glove will fit what I say."

"Who shot you?" Sergeant Conlon asked.

"The boss himself," Schultz answered

"What did he shoot you for?"

"I showed him, boss. Did you hear me meet him? An appointment. Appeal stuck. All right, Mother."

"Was it the boss that shot you?"

"Who shot me? No one."

"What did they shoot you for?"

"I don't know, sir. Honestly, I don't. I don't even know who was with me, honestly. I went to the toilet. I was in the toilet and when I reached the—the boy came at me."

"The big fellow gave it to you?"

"No. I don't know who shot me. Pardon me, I forgot. I forgot that I am a plaintiff and not a defendant. Look out. Look out for him, please! He owes me money. He owes everyone money. Why can't he just pull out and give me control? No! No! A boy has never wept nor dashed a thousand kim."

Conlon asked again, "Who shot you?"

"I don't know."

"How many shots were fired?"

"A thousand."

As the delirium continued, Schultz's wife appeared at her husband's bedside. "This is Frances, Arthur," she said.

"Who shot you?" asked Conlon once again.

"I don't know. I didn't even get a look. I don't know who could have done it. Anybody. Kindly take my shoes off."

"They are off."

"No. There's a handcuff on them. Look out for Jimmy Valentine, for he is an old pal of mine. Come on, come on, Jim. Okay, okay, I'm all through."

At 8:40 p.m.—at the conclusion of his strangely poetic deathbed dissertation, Arthur Flegenheimer, alias Dutch Schultz, gave up the ghost.

POTATOES KAUFMAN AND THE CARPET JOINTS

Julian Kaufman had cornered the market on potatoes futures in Chicago. That's how he came to be known as Potatoes. Like many young city guys, he was drawn to the world of bootlegging and gambling. That world, Chicago style, was even more wild and treacherous than the one that existed in the parallel universe of New York.

Now, Potatoes was in big trouble. He had been living dangerously as a member of the notorious Dion O'Bannion gang. By 1928, Kaufman and his partner, Bugs Moran, were co-owners of the Sheridan Wave Tournament Club, the ritziest casino in Chicago. Moran, had a long-time feud going between himself and Scarface Al Capone, and several years later, he would mow down Capone's henchman, Machine Gun Jack McGurn, as retribution for McGurn's masterminding of the St. Valentine's Day Massacre, in which six of Moran's men were executed.

In the spring of 1930, Jake Lingle, a corrupt reporter for the *Chicago Tribune* and pal of Al Capone's, attempted to extort money from Kaufman and Moran. Lingle was shot dead as he scanned the Daily Racing Form he had just purchased from a sidewalk newsstand. The brazen killing of a civilian created a public outrage that pissed off Capone, who held Bugs Moran responsible for creating a lot of heat. Capone let it be known that he would avenge the killing come Hell or High Water. A contract was put out on both Moran and Kaufman.

Potatoes fled to New York, where he found his way to Jimmy Blue Eyes. Jimmy had enough clout to put the word out that Kaufman was under his protection.

Not only was Julian grateful to Jimmy for the protection he'd provided, but he had found a good and true friend. After the repeal of the Volstead Act, Jimmy was looking for another way to make a buck. Julian Kaufman would provide the solution and, although they didn't know it at the time, would open the door to a cleaner, better, *and safer* life for all of them.

IN THE WINTER OF 1934, Julian said to Jimmy, "Pack your bags. I wanna show you something."

Right after Christmas, the two men began a leisurely motor trip down the east coast, laughing and kibitzing as they traveled south from state to state. Once they reached Georgia, the terrain began to change noticeably. They spent the night at a roadside cabin, had grits and eggs for breakfast and continued on their journey. They shed their sweaters as the temperature rose.

As they drove on, they saw the first coconut palms, their long fronds swaying in the breeze along the narrow ocean highway. This was not the familiar Atlantic Ocean of Long Island or the Jersey shore. This was white sand and open spaces.

Julian's hands rested lightly on the steering wheel. "You'll see, Jimmy, it's a new frontier down here. It's wide open."

Jimmy breathed in the warm salt air and felt the tropical heat on his arm as it rested on the open window of the roadster. He was thirty years old and ripe for a new beginning in the land of eternal sunshine.

THE FLORIDA real estate boom began to take off in the early Twenties and escalated into a frenzy of marketing, building, and buying. An advertisement in a Florida publication, The Miamian, in an orgy of hyperbole, waxed poetic:

> *Where you sit and watch at twilight the fronds of the graceful palm,*
>
> *Latticed against the fading gold of the sun-kissed sky—*
>
> *Where the whispering breeze springs fresh from the lap of the Caribbean*
>
> *And woes with elusive cadence like unto a mother's lullaby....*

Buses brought prospective investors to watch the dredging and steam shoveling that was to convert the mangrove swamps into a gorgeous Venetian paradise. The Old Dixie Highway was clogged with travelers. Hotels were jammed. People were migrating by the droves to Miami Beach and Coral Gables and the entire strip of coastline from Palm Beach southward was being touted as America's answer to the Riviera.

What Julian wanted Jimmy to see was the town of Hollywood-By-The-Sea and neighboring Hallandale. Hollywood-By-The-Sea (as it was called back in the day) was peppered with Mediterranean-style mansions that featured stucco walls and cross-gabled red tile roofs. There were also charming, whitewashed bungalows and wooden Florida shotgun cottages scattered among the pinewoods and the palmettos. Purple bougainvillea and red hibiscus dotted the streets, which were patriotically named after American presidents.

Hallandale, a farming community with a tiny population, was the closest thing to a new frontier to be found on the eastern seaboard. It was there that Julian had discovered the rough-and-tumble "sawdust joints" run by area locals; and, it was there that he had staked his claim and established the Old Plantation Club on Hallandale Boulevard, a two-lane road that ran from Old Dixie Highway to the ocean. Julian had the idea that the area was ripe for development. Jimmy agreed and thought that Meyer would as well.

Since Potatoes Kaufman had been at the helm of Chicago's Sheridan Wave Tournament Club, he was convinced that the "sawdust joints" of Hallandale could be replaced by "carpet joints" that would attract wealthy tourists and high rollers. As soon as Jimmy brought Meyer onboard, they went into action. The Old Plantation would continue to attract a steady clientele—but the three partners were on to bigger and better things.

Meyer had discovered his niche when he turned his attention from bootlegging to the running of two up-scale casinos in Saratoga Springs, New York: the Arrowhead Inn and the Piping Rock, which he co-owned with partners, Frank Costello and Joe Adonis.

In Saratoga, Meyer's cool, quiet demeanor established an immediate sense of order and class. But what served him best was his reputation for scrupulous honesty. He made it clear that cheating on the part of the dealers would not be tolerated. Business was to be run strictly on the up and up.

Meyer loved the gaming rooms with wealthy clientele leaning over well-appointed tables lined with green felt. As he watched them stacking their chips, tossing dice, clutching their cards at the twenty-one tables or gazing expectantly at the turn of the roulette wheel, he could relax in the knowledge that the odds were, just naturally, going to be on the side of the house.

Flo in front of Hollywood Country Club Circa 1934

The Hollywood Country Club with its Moorish architecture surrounded by coconut and date palms, contained a nightclub (complete with a rooftop that slid back to reveal open sky above the stage and orchestra) plus a restaurant and a casino. In the

Twenties, it had been owned and operated by none other than Al Capone. Now, Julian, Jimmy, and Meyer, along with a few other investors, prepared to rejuvenate the property and turn it into a stylish, top-notch "carpet joint."

Jimmy and Julian found a bungalow to rent at 1809 Dewey Street; and, before long, Flo and Julian's wife, Marion, boarded a train at Pennsylvania Station and arrived the following day at the rustic little Hollywood Station on Old Dixie Highway. Jimmy and Julian were there to pick them up. They piled into a waiting roadster and it took less than ten minutes to arrive at the rented bungalow.

Inside, it was filled with bamboo furniture and the floors were covered with shiny brown Cuban tiles. There was a fireplace for those rare nights when warmth was required; but mostly, the nights were balmy and the open windows invited the fragrance of night-blooming jasmine to fill the rooms. None of them knew then that Florida was to become their second home.

The Alos and the Kaufmans spent the next few months enjoying the little cottage, which was owned by Joe Lolly, the golf pro at the country club who encouraged Jimmy and Flo to take up golf. As workmen labored over the renovations, various visitors from New York showed up to see what was going on. It was the beginning of a trend that would continue—a parade of friends and family coming down, each year, to winter in Florida for *the season*.

Jimmy and Flo continued their pursuit of golf under the tutelage of Joe Lolly. Meyer and his wife, Ann, arrived in Hollywood for the first time. The women enjoyed the weather, the beach, and each other's company, while the men concentrated on business.

Jimmy and Meyer immediately set about making connections in town and greasing the palms of local officials. Meyer's brother,

Jake, came down to oversee the continuing operation of the Old Plantation in Hallandale. Contributions to local organizations such as the Elks, the Shriners and local hospitals spread good will and quieted any complaints coming from the local citizenry. Payoffs were forthcoming to Broward County politicians and law-enforcement officials—most notably, Sheriff Walter Clark, who "set the right example" by looking the other way to the extent that, by 1940, there would be illegal slot machines in virtually every coffee shop and drugstore in the area.

By January of 1935, the partners were ready to launch their first "carpet joint" in Florida. For the grand opening, they brought in the extremely popular Xaviar Cougat and his orchestra. Later that first season, there was Harry Richman, Paul Whiteman, and the comedian, Joe E. Lewis. The final star of the season was Sophie Tucker (the most famous of the old "coon-shouters" from vaudeville days). In the evenings, Jimmy and Flo could hear the singer through their windows, her full-bodied voice floating in from the open-air stage a block away.

Their life was coming into full swing. Both Jimmy and Meyer had been searching, not only for a new source of revenue—but also for a new beginning. Whatever they had done or seen done or known to be done, up until now, might with a little luck, fade from memory. They had navigated through the rough seas of Prohibition and lived to tell about it.

Jimmy felt like the luckiest guy in the world. A mere eight years ago, he had walked out of Dannemora Prison. Now, he was poised to become a major player in the development of the fledgling gaming industry in Florida—which would prove to be of great benefit to the growth of South Florida as a tourist mecca.

Jimmy on boat in Florida

When we first got there in 1932, there were fifteen hundred people living in Hallandale. Everybody in town was busted in those days. I went to see the sheriff, Walter Clark. He was a good old boy, sittin' with his feet up on the desk and his fingers in his suspenders. A real nice guy. He'd steal a red-hot stove. Those politicians, you could buy them with a ham sandwich. If we corrupted them, they wanted to be corrupted. We were lucky. It was the Depression and nobody had any money but us. We spread it around—and it made us very popular.

WHO IS MY MOTHER?

On a stifling July morning in 1941, when Flo got the call that her sister, Grace, had given birth, she rushed to St. Claire's Hospital, in the theatre district of Manhattan. Since Jimmy was in Hot Springs taking the mineral baths, she was accompanied by her sidekick, a chubby, moon-faced character by the name of Louie Levine.

Flo had lost a baby girl during the time that my mother was carrying me—and, although she wasn't usually given to flights of fancy, when the nurse put me into her arms, she turned to Louie and said, "I know this baby." She would tell the story over and over again as I grew. In this way, I understood that she believed there was a special bond between us.

Four months later, on a Sunday morning, the news came that Japan had bombed Pearl Harbor. That brought America into the war, which had already been raging in Europe for two years. Uncle Jim, who was thirty-seven at the time, tried to join up. Decades later, amongst his papers, I would find a letter from the War

Department dated September 9, 1942, rejecting his request to join the Signal Corps. Maybe they rejected him based on his age. Or maybe it was because he was a convicted felon. He must have been calling the War Department every kind of "rat-bastard" when he got that letter.

Mother

Anyway, life went on. Everybody focused on the daily news bulletins from overseas. People were buying war bonds like crazy and worrying about their loved ones being shipped out to foreign shores. My aunt's two sons, Larry and Billy, joined up and she handled it with her usual stoicism. Stiff upper lip and all that.

With my arrival and all the chaos and confusion of the war, my uncle and aunt stayed in New York to celebrate Christmas before packing their bags and heading south that year. A month later, my mother followed, taking me for my first ride on the Eastern Seaboard Railroad. My aunt, who I would always call Auntie Doe, and my grandmother met us in their summer print dresses, surrounded by the colorful crotons that grew against the station walls in Hollywood. Hattie, the black woman who worked for my uncle and aunt as housekeeper and cook, accompanied them. Hattie immediately folded me into her welcoming arms and smiled broadly at the camera as my aunt took snapshots to commemorate the occasion.

The following January, my mother again brought me to Florida for a month's vacation. Later that summer, back in New York, she and my aunt launched a business venture together. With Uncle Jim's financial backing, my mother opened the Carole Rita Beauty Salon on the second floor of a building overlooking Columbus Circle. My mother, as the working partner, managed the shop. I have fragmented memories of playing on the floor as my petit, freckle-faced mother bustled around the place, her platform shoes clicking along the floor, her strawberry-blond hair combed into a stylish upsweep. When I was around two years old, a nanny was hired to care for me. She was nothing like Hattie, who was warm and loving and smelled like Juicy Fruit chewing gum and on whose ample bosom I could nestle. My mother soon discovered that the nanny was punishing me by putting me into a dark closet. When my aunt and uncle heard about this, they offered to take me down south for a few months, while my mother was busy with the shop.

To her later, eternal regret, my mother agreed.

Hattie, Grandmother, and baby Carole at the Hollywood Train Station

Although Uncle Jim would become my surrogate father, it wasn't as if I didn't have an actual one. Benjamin Contrada (AKA Banjo) was a classic Broadway character. He was rough around the edges and, apparently, my mother, twelve years his junior, married him for "security." Though he may have seemed easygoing to her in the beginning, a few years into the relationship he would prove to be less pliable than my mother had thought.

Banjo

My father was born in Naples, Italy, in 1897, and grew up in New Rochelle, New York, amongst a tribe of twelve brothers and sisters. At sixteen, he lied about his age and joined the army to escape a miserable relationship with his father, who enjoyed hitting the bottle and the kids. Just before the onset of World War I, he was released—and decided to give prizefighting a try.

He was a flyweight and he earned a pretty good reputation traveling around the country, particularly on the West Coast, where he was known as Kid Browning. He was quick on his feet and continued fighting for several years, until someone finally landed a good one to his kisser, smashing his nose into a new shape. It was then that he decided the fight game was not for him.

He went to night school, where he studied calculus and, utilizing his strong ability in mathematics, became an expert tool and die maker. It was a living, but he soon discovered that working a nine-to-five job didn't suit him. The legitimate world didn't offer him the "action" that he craved. His mathematical talent could also come in handy in the gambling trade. He found he could get along bankrolling and running crap games and living by his wits.

For a time, Banjo had a room in the Piccadilly Hotel, a popular show business and underworld hangout on West Forty-Fifth Street, where he kept a dog and a small monkey. In the evenings, when he left them alone, the dog would chase the monkey or the monkey would chase the dog and they made a hell of a racket. A woman living down the hall complained to the front desk that it sounded like my father had wild animals in his room. He began getting daily calls about the monkey—but he insisted that he didn't know what the caller meant. Eventually, he discovered that the calls were not coming from the hotel manager, but from a Broadway producer who needed a monkey to perform in his show. The monkey got the job and earned his keep for months.

In 1938, when my uncle and aunt heard that Grace was marrying Banjo, they were stunned. As for my father, in his line of work it didn't hurt that he was becoming the brother-in-law of Jimmy Blue Eyes. In fact, my father thought of Jimmy as his ace-in-the-hole.

After their marriage, my father's habits didn't change much. He seemed to be in his own world. On a gray January day, my father and my aunt were on their way to visit my mother who was in the hospital with a case of food poisoning. As they tramped through a heavy layer of snow, my aunt tripped and fell into a snowdrift. Completely oblivious, my father kept walking while my aunt was left to pick herself up. She fumed as she dusted off the snow and rushed to catch up with him, shouting a few choice names at the back of his head.

On another occasion, a man wielding a gun approached my father on the street. The man knew my father and was aware that he always carried a large bankroll.

"Okay, Banjo, hand over your money," the man demanded.

"No," said my father.

With that, the bungling bandit fired a shot. The bullet went between my father's legs, where it entered and exited harmlessly through his overcoat. Several weeks later, my father was walking down the street when he ran into a detective he knew.

"For Christ's sake, Banjo," the cop yelled at him, "You're walking around with bullet holes in your coat!" Absent-minded as ever, it hadn't occurred to my father to buy a new coat.

AFTER THE FIRST FEW YEARS, my parents were basically leading separate lives. As far as I can recall, they never went anywhere together. They definitely had very different eating habits. When he cooked hot cherry peppers, fiery fumes filled the apartment and made breathing impossible. (My mother and I would flee, only able to return hours later, when the smoke had cleared.) He then added the peppers to everything he ate for the rest of the week. "Banjo has a cast-iron stomach," Uncle Jim would say, laughing.

My father made pitchers of fresh lemonade and salads topped with salty anchovies. From Little Italy, he brought home fragrant Genoa salami and chunks of Provolone cheese. My mother complained that by the time he was through in the kitchen, olive oil covered every doorknob.

My mother favored a more Irish, or, at least, American table. Stews. Meat and potatoes. Baked macaroni. However, on Sundays, she made a red sauce with delicious meatballs or chicken (a skill learned during a brief teenage marriage to an Italian boy). But when my father made a sauce, he used big, fresh clams and grated his own cheese. My mother found all of this terribly aggravating. Why did my father have to be so—*Italian?*

She refused to share a bathroom with him and left his bathroom undecorated, with plain white towels that suffered from the gray imprint of the daily newspapers he read. In contrast, the bathroom that I shared with my mother was large and inviting and adorned with charming wallpaper—multi-colored bubbles floating towards the ceiling.

My mother said that she couldn't go to a restaurant with my father because of his manners.

He attacked his food, oil dribbling down his chin. "He eats as if he was raised in a barn," she would say. She couldn't stand the loudness and gruffness of his voice. He was uncouth. Even his walk, an odd side-to-side shuffle (which I could imitate to perfection) seemed to set him apart as an object of ridicule in the eyes of the family.

When he was angry, my father's voice resembled the sound of a roaring bear. But my five-foot mother was the fearless animal tamer. One of her favorite weapons was a machete that Cousin

Billy had removed from the body of a Japanese soldier. She would chase my father around the apartment, brandishing the machete in the air. Although he was capable of infuriating her to the point where she lost all control, he regarded her maniacal attacks with a remarkable amount of good humor. While she seemed to *tolerate* him—he clearly *adored* her.

"Look at her," he would say, good-naturedly, as she bustled around the apartment, a cigarette dangling from her mouth. "Look at the Madame. Did you know she murdered her first two husbands?" (After her short-lived teen marriage, my mother had been married to a Jewish hat maker, Benny Bernstein, who succumbed to tuberculosis, probably brought on from inhaling too much felt.) She seemed to pay no attention to the things he said. His humor escaped her.

There were always battles about money. My mother said that getting her weekly house allowance was "like pulling teeth." But later, the major cause of her resentment would become the issue of "the baby." Namely, me.

THE ATMOSPHERE in Florida with my uncle and aunt was far different from my parents' home. I can't recall my uncle or aunt ever raising their voices to each other. Uncle Jim, Aunty Doe and I were together every day at the beach, where they had a cabana at the Hollywood Beach Hotel. Sometimes we would go to the Monkey Jungle, where colorfully clad Seminole Indians wrestled with alligators, and there was a chimpanzee named Oona O'Neill. They told me that was the name of Charlie Chaplin's wife.

Jimmy and baby Carole

One day stands out indelibly in my mind. I'm about three years old, tall enough to stand on the front seat of Uncle Jim's brand new Cadillac. He's going to take my aunt and me for a drive. I'm holding an ice cream cone and I remember thinking *I'm gonna put this ice cream into my hand.* Naturally, it drips right through my pudgy little fingers all over the seat. Uncle Jim is not pleased. He pulls into a parking space in front of the barbershop where he goes in the morning for a shave. He and Aunty Doe get out and leave me in the car. They're standing on the curb underneath a palm tree and Uncle Jim has his hands on his hips and a big grin on his face. I'm crying and screaming and slapping my hands against the window—throwing one hell of a tantrum—and he's getting a kick out of it. I guess he thought he was teaching me a lesson about the ice cream. So the first thing I remember in my life is helplessness, injustice, and being *really* pissed off.

While Uncle Jim was out every night taking care of business, my aunt was left to amuse herself with friends. She was approaching forty and had everything money could buy. But the two sons she hadn't raised were in harm's way overseas. The baby she had lost would be the last she would ever conceive. She had an emptiness that needed to be filled.

I absorbed everything about her: Indian-black hair; long and parted in the center. Smooth, pale skin. Straight nose. Gold-flecked eyes. Strong hands tipped with long, red-lacquered nails. Her footsteps were quick. She smelled of Arpege.

I remember Uncle Jim as a moving object. Holding his hand. Driving in his car. I remember the shoes that he wore, lined up in the closet like works of art: Pointy-toed with perforations. Two-toned. Suede with flaps. Uncle Jim looked like the epitome of a gangster. Straight from Central Casting.

As children, my aunt and my mother, raven-haired Flo and freckle-faced little Gracie clung to each other and to their mother, Grace Kane, a tall, handsome redhead. When she was abandoned by her husband, ne`er-do-well Anthony Gesualdi, Grace moved her daughters into the Irish neighborhood where they felt deep shame when they heard Italians referred to as Wops, Guinnies, and Greaseballs. Although both girls would eventually marry Italian men, they thought of themselves as Irish, through and through. In due course, my grandmother married Harry Gelinas, a stern, silent Frenchman, The family lived on Long Island where they struggled with poverty.

Flo and Grace

But all that was in the past and now Grace and Flo were glamour girls. They bought their undergarments from a man called Baghdad. I remember him coming to my parents' apartment in the summertime, carrying his merchandise—silk nightgowns, slips, panties, bras—in a battered brown leather suitcase. I would sit on the floor and watch as he lifted the treasures— soft, shimmery garments trimmed with ribbons and buttons and laces—ceremoniously from his bag. While my mother and aunt fussed and decided, I listened to Baghdad speak shyly, in an odd accent, of a book he was writing about Jesus. Uncle Jim, an avowed atheist, privately scoffed at such talk and said that Baghdad was "a nut."

I'M FOUR OR FIVE. My aunt and I descend steep staircases and climb aboard the Florida East Coast Limited. All the trains have names. The Miamian, the Champion, the Florida Special. They're like powerful, heaving, giant beasts. Elephants. Or dinosaurs.

The excitement of travel distracts me from any feelings of separation. Aunty Doe takes off her hat and shoes, puts on slippers, and we settle into our compartment. Soon, the tall black porter brings our lunch, which he sets down on a table that appears, as if by magic, from the wall. We order club sandwiches with potato chips and ginger ale.

Auntie Doe puts her feet up, sips a cup of coffee, and tries to work on a crossword puzzle. Now, we are completely out of the city and, together, we search the passing landscape for a glimpse of a horse or cow. Later, we lurch our way to the dining car, where my aunt writes our order on a small pad and hands it to the waiter. Later still, the porter returns to our room. He opens the bottom bed, which is constructed from the seat. The top bunk comes out of the wall, complete with blankets, sheets, and pillows. The porter bids us a pleasant evening in a deep, melodious voice.

In our nightclothes, Auntie Doe and I snuggle into our beds and I can feel the motion of the train and hear the chug, chug, chug of the wheels on the track. For the moment, the warm glow of the lamps and the coziness of the cabin create feelings of deep contentment.

As we speed through the darkness to a world dotted by palm trees and drenched with sun—a world in which my uncle and aunt predominate—my mother's absence recedes into the background on the screen of my mind.

Carole

MONROE STREET

At the end of the summer of 1946, when my uncle and aunt heard that my mother had enrolled me in first grade in New York, there was a big blowout in the family. Uncle Jim urged my father to let me come to Florida, explaining that my aunt had become very attached to me.

In November, I traveled south with Aunty Doe. I would never attend a New York school again.

My mother always told me that my father, aunt, and uncle *steamrolled* her—*"tortured"* her into sending me to Florida. She often used that word.

"In the end," she said, "I gave up."

Later, when I began to question the arrangement of our lives, they would all have their stories.

"They stole you," my mother said.

"We were your godparents. We rescued you," was the way Uncle Jim put it.

"Your uncle came to me with tears in his eyes and begged me to let you go to Florida," my father explained, as he dabbed at the tears in his own eyes with a handkerchief.

We were at the starting line of a tug-of-war in which I would be the rope.

AUNTY DOE and I arrived in Florida that November to the newly constructed house on Monroe Street. Uncle Jim was already there —involved with the day-to-day operations of a handful of casinos. Aunty Doe's job was to complete the interior of the house with the aid of her decorator, Ada Tamor—a delightful old lady who had once been an apprentice to the legendary designer, Elsie de Wolfe.

VINCENT ALO'S HOME IS AT 1248 MONROE ST.

The daily routine quickly fell into place with Hattie running the household. Wearing a white uniform and crisp, white apron, she presided over the red and white kitchen where she produced delicious meals for the family: fried chicken with corn fritters, deep dishes of creamy baked macaroni, icy fresh lemonade served in a silver pitcher, breakfasts of pancakes stacked high, and grapefruits and oranges straight off the trees behind the kitchen.

Hollywood, Florida, in the forties seemed idyllic. The town itself was small, reaching from the Atlantic Ocean, across the intercoastal waterway and eighteen blocks west to Old Dixie Highway. Bursts of color from purple bougainvillea complemented the bungalows and villas. Coconut or royal palms, accented by the blooms of hibiscus and oleander growing along white sidewalks, studded the streets. The overall effect was one of simplicity and charm.

Jimmy and Carole on the handball court in Hollywood

Everyone who was anyone in the gambling trade kept a cabana at the Hollywood Beach Hotel, which stood, in all its pink majesty, on the ocean at the end of Hollywood Boulevard. Day after sun-drenched day, the wives lounged around the hotel pool and socialized, while the children splashed and swam in the Olympic-sized pool. The courts where the men played handball stood on the beach itself, just yards away from the flowing surf. Sometimes, Auntie Doe would play with Uncle Jim and Meyer or with her faithful sidekick, Louie Levine.

Meyer's brother, Jake, was part of the management of the Colonial Inn, and his wife, Ann, was always at the pool with her daughter, Linda, who was my favorite playmate. Potatoes Kaufman had passed away, but his wife, Marion, was very much a part of the scene. Louie Levine lived in a small cottage behind her 1920s Spanish hacienda on Harrison Street.

At home, there was constant activity with an endless stream of friends coming by to hold court with Uncle Jim. My favorite was jovial Hy Gynnis, who owned a Chicago nightclub called the Tradewinds, and his blonde, beautiful wife, Kay. He invented an alter ego for me, named Sophie. Whenever I acted like a brat, Hy would say, "Listen, Carole didn't do that. It was Sophie. Yeah, Sophie. That's right. She's hiding under the table right now." He even had *me* believing in Sophie. "Boy!" he would say, laughing, "I sure feel sorry for the poor guy who winds up marrying Sophie."

Jimmy, Flo, Betty & George Wood

Gregarious George Wood, the hotshot representative from New York's William Morris Theatrical Agency showed up frequently.

He was Uncle Jim's close pal and he supplied the star power for the Colonial Inn.

There were characters like Adele Howe, ex-girlfriend of Owney Madden (called the English Godfather, Madden operated New York's Cotton Club in the 1920s.) In her throaty voice, Adele would tell stories. She was a "booster." I enjoyed her tales about how she could walk out of a store with a typewriter between her legs—or enter a furrier's showroom so regally that the sales personnel never questioned the fur that left the store on her arm.

There were the regulars, like Mildred and Billy Burns, ex-vaudevillians who were always on hand for holiday meals and who taught me how to tap dance.

Good-natured, cigar-smoking Louie Levine was a daily presence at the house. A New York taxi driver, he had never been out of the city when he was discovered by my uncle, who took childlike Louie under his wing. For the remainder of his life, Uncle Jim would look after him—and he would reciprocate by worshiping my uncle, whom he called "Chief." He was my aunt's devoted sidekick, and referred to her, lovingly, as "Partner."

My uncle and aunt's friends were larger than life and fun to be around. In those days before television, people had more interactive ways of entertaining themselves. As a kid of five or six, I enjoyed the company of the adults and was always "on the earie," as they used to say. I was on hand for the card-playing, kibitzing, and good-natured high-jinks that went on in the evenings in the comfortable Florida room overlooking South Lake.

Thursdays and Sundays were family nights out in our household. Twice a week, I would climb into the back seat of the Cadillac. Aunty Doe would be seated in front of me, all decked out. Uncle Jim would be at the wheel, navigating through the early evening light with the intensity of Sea Biscuit crossing the finish line—and we would be off to one of the clubs.

I'd hang my head out the window to catch the wind, but I could still hear the radio and Walter Winchell, rapping out, in his trademark staccato, "Good evening, Mr. and Mrs. America—and all the ships at sea! Let's go to press!"

I clearly remember the Greenacres— a simple, rustic structure standing in the middle of a Florida pine forest. The exterior was simple and quaint, and in the dining room, the tables were covered with pristine white cloths. Thick steaks were served there, along with Shirley Temple cocktails. In the casino, I was allowed to stand on a chair and pull the arm of a slot machine, amid all the exciting hubbub. After dinner, there was a dance band and my uncle and aunt would glide smoothly around the floor together like Ginger Rogers and Fred Astaire.

The Colonial Inn was very different. The driveway led up to an imposing building fronted by white columns and wide steps. The interior was sheer elegance. Bernardo, the suave and charming maître d' would greet us with, "Hello, Meester Jeemie," and escort us to our ringside table in the showroom, where we were treated like royalty by waiters who brought delicacies like giant shrimp hanging around an ice-filled cup and lamb chops wearing paper doilies.

"Say," Uncle Jim would call to a waiter, "will you send the cigarette girl over here? And the camera girl—she can take a couple a pictures. And bring the baby a Shirley Temple."

At some point during dinner, the floorshow would begin. Tall, beautiful ladies paraded around the stage in costumes made of plumes, sequins, feathers, and beads. Next, there would always be a ballroom dancing couple swirling around the stage to usher in the opening act.

Carole with a Showgirl at the Colonial Inn

I sat in Carmen Miranda's dressing room and waited as she took off her hatful of bananas. Then I showed her my appendix scar and she showed me hers.

When the curtain rose and Jane Froman stood in front of the piano singing *With a Song in My Heart*, the audience had no idea that she was being held erect by a platform hidden beneath her flowing gown. (She had lost a leg in a plane crash during the war.)

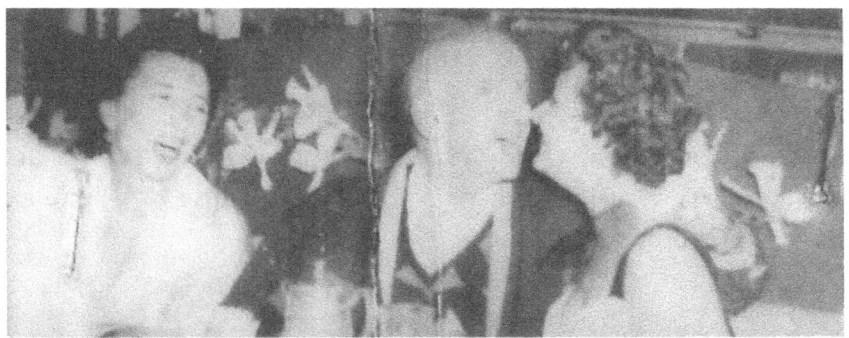

Flo with Durante

When Jimmy Durante tore up the piano, creating his unique brand of mayhem onstage— or Joe E. Lewis ruefully sang, "Sam, You Made the Pants Too Long," producing waves of laughter. *That was something special.* Young as I was, I recognized magic when I saw it. I had the impression that the stars who appeared on stage were more than mere mortals. They were magicians who turned everyday reality into stardust.

Uncle Jim presided over these exciting places where waiters, sequined cigarette girls, maître d's in their tuxedos hovered around, murmuring, *Mr. Jimmy*, this—and *Mr. Jimmy*, that. Where women wore upswept hair, and loads of diamonds, and cocktail dresses with big skirts in silk or taffeta. Where delicious food was served—and famous performers sang and danced, and they were nice to you and made you laugh.

One day, the news came on the radio and someone was talking about Uncle Jim. That's how I learned that my uncle was sometimes called "Blue Eyes," which seemed ridiculous to me, since he clearly didn't have blue eyes.

Like all children, I accepted the circumstances of our life as completely normal. I mean, didn't every kid have an Auntie Adele, who could walk out of a store with a typewriter in her bloomers?

Even as I grew and became more conscious of my uncle's public reputation, it didn't concern me. The person I knew bore no resemblance to newspaper reports or the claims of politicians. Only decades later would I confront the contradiction of his private persona against what little I could glimpse of a hidden, darker facet of my uncle's life.

BYE, BYE, BUGSY

Sometime during the summer of 1947, Uncle Jim was arrested in New York; and though he had three hundred and thirty-six dollars in his pocket at the time, he was charged with vagrancy. The police wanted to find out what he knew about the murder of a waterfront labor leader by the name of Anthony Hintz.

One of the suspects being held in connection to the crime was "Cockeye" Johnny Dunn. Dunn was the brother-in-law of Eddie McGrath, a waterfront boss and childhood friend of Jimmy Blue Eyes.

"I don't know anything about it. If they want to kill somebody, that's their business," Uncle Jim told the cops.

Johnny Dunn was convicted of the gangland slaying, held in Sing Sing on death row, and executed in the electric chair. Uncle Jim was greatly affected by this and would always maintain Dunn's innocence.

In the same year, Uncle Jim's old friend, Ben Siegel, was murdered while sitting on the chintz couch in the living room of his girlfriend, Virginia Hill.

When Prohibition had ended, Ben Siegel had migrated west to Los Angeles where he hobnobbed with celebrities and entertained the idea of getting into the picture business. Having left his wife, Esther, behind in New York, he focused on escorting starlets around and making as dazzling an impression as he could in Hollywood's Café Society.

He began a relationship with Virginia Hill, a tough broad, who had been part of the scene back in New York and was familiar with all "the boys." Virginia was a good-time girl; but when she hooked up with Ben, it seemed to be the real thing for both of them. She was with him from the beginning, as he sought to create something new and fabulous in the desert of Las Vegas, Nevada.

Siegel proved himself a visionary when he took over the reins of the Flamingo Hotel from Billy Wilkerson, creator of two of Hollywood's favorite hotspots, Ciro's and Café Trocadero.

When Wilkerson ran out of money shortly after construction began, Siegel, along with other partners, including Meyer, was able to buy into the project and secure a majority holding in the hotel.

With Virginia Hill by his side, he undertook the construction of the Flamingo and rushed to complete it on schedule by Christmas 1946. Jimmy Durante topped the bill and opened the nightclub, along with Rose Marie and the Xavier Cugat band.

Although the casino, dining room, and showroom were striking and no expense had been spared in outfitting them, the hotel itself was not completed so there were no paying guests. That, along with kinks that hadn't been ironed out at the gaming tables, caused a financial free fall. Clearly, the opening had been premature and ill-advised. The Flamingo Hotel closed one month after it had opened.

It's said that Ben Siegel traveled to Florida to beg Meyer and Company to help with his cash-flow problem. Harold Conrad, the legendary New York press agent of the era, reported a scene that allegedly took place one evening at the Colonial Inn. A customer approached Siegel and greeted him, "Hi, Bugsy!" not knowing that he had just committed the cardinal sin of addressing him by the nickname he despised. Ben punched the man and knocked him to the floor. "Ben Siegel is the name," he yelled, "and don't you ever forget it." Then he kicked the unfortunate man in the ribs for good measure. Frank Costello, who was standing by, commented dryly, "That's very bad manners, Ben. You should'a never kicked him."

With Meyer Lansky, Frank Costello, and Jimmy Blue Eyes in his corner, Ben was given the money to complete the Flamingo, even though other partners involved in bankrolling the project were skeptical. The hotel reopened on March 1, 1947, with the Andrew Sisters heading the bill in the showroom. At this point, Siegel attempted to buy out Wilkerson's 33-percent of the Flamingo. During a negotiation over price, he lost his famous temper and threatened Wilkerson's life. When Wilkerson's attorney told Siegel that he was filing an affidavit concerning the threats that had been made, Ben reportedly went ballistic.

At the time of his murder in Beverly Hills on the night of June 20th, Siegel's West Coast partners were Gus Greenbaum, Moe Sedway, Davie Berman, and several others. He had spent a good deal of their money. With Siegel, the loose cannon, out of the way, they were able to obtain a large bank loan and keep the hotel solvent. They became the new bosses of the Flamingo.

Many sources have suggested that Siegel's death was ordered or, at least, approved by Meyer. That would also involve my uncle, given his close association with Meyer. Nothing can convince me that Meyer and Jimmy had anything to do with the death of Ben Siegel. They were his close friends. Perhaps they had to stand by and let nature take its course. Siegel had stepped on a lot of toes. Years later when I asked my uncle about Ben Siegel's death, he said that Ben had given Virginia a vicious beating several days before; and he believed her enraged younger brother, Chick Hill, had avenged his sister.

My father had a photograph of Siegel, slouched on a couch, his eyes blown out of his head. I think he got it from a detective he knew at the time. When I was nine or ten, I saw that photo. It was pretty gruesome. Maybe I came across it. Or, just as likely, my father showed it to me. So much for appropriate parenting.

I never met Ben Siegel. But I clearly remember dinner table conversations in which he was discussed. I recall my aunt mentioning him. How handsome he was. How charming. They talked about his wife, Esther, and his daughter, Millicent. I thought of him as a family friend. Nobody ever brought up the terrible way his life ended.

It's hard to reconcile the seemingly contradictory aspects of my uncle's life. Friends and acquaintances were occasionally killed around him, casting a sinister shadow that remained just out of sight. On the other hand, Uncle Jim, with his calm and tranquil manner was the Rock of Gibraltar at the center of our universe.

I ATTENDED the Helen Hart Private School in a three-room house on Hollywood Boulevard. School hours were 9:00 till 12:00. In those days, before air conditioning, people came and went with the seasons. Since that brought us to Florida in November and we left in April, my early education seems primitive. Nobody seemed too concerned about the abbreviated number of hours I spent in school.

Carole

Occasionally, some of the beautiful showgirls from the Colonial Inn came to our house. They would lounge with their long legs draped over the living room furniture or sit cross-legged on the floor while we listened to a recording my aunt had of *Manhattan Towers*, Gordon Jenkin's narrative love-letter to New York. I had been dancing since age three, and the girls would ask me to put on my point shoes and they would twirl around the living room and dance with me.

I suppose I enjoyed my life in Florida, but the visits from my mother—who arrived ceremoniously with her luggage and her cocker spaniel, Suzy, and disappeared again after a few weeks— were jarring. I awaited her appearances and grieved her departures. After six months in Florida with my aunt and uncle, I would be transported back to another world. Back to New York and to my real parents. I found it difficult to switch gears—often calling my aunt "Mommy" and my mother "Aunty Doe."

In the summer of 1947, my grandmother died. In spite of the growing tension between my mother and my aunt, they united in grief over the loss of their mother.

The Carole Rita Beauty Salon had folded, and the frequent trips my mother could now take to Florida had to compensate for her loss of dominion regarding my upbringing. When she showed up, she shared my bedroom and seemed to have reduced herself from parent to sibling.

The summers spent in New York with my mother and father, however, shine in my mind. To me, the coziness of my parents' apartment easily trumped the house in Florida with its servants and silver dinner bells. Florida dimmed in comparison to the splendor that was New York. The honking of horns, the clacking of horses' hoofs in Central Park, the cacophony of sounds from the streets—the air itself seemed to vibrate with energy. My mother took me to the movies, to Horn and Hardart's cafeteria, where pies came out of glass cubicles in the wall and you sometimes shared your table with strangers.

I attended Charlie Lowe's, the crème de la crème of children's dancing schools alongside talented kids like the Heinz Brothers.

My ballet teacher, Lee Dearring, became very close to my mother, and her five-year-old daughter, Mary Lee, who was a child actress, became my New York best friend.

In spite of my mother and father's fierce arguments, I thought my father was fun. He'd put me on his shoulders and run through the apartment yelling, "Madame! Quick, get a knife. There's something growing on my neck." He took me to see the same Danny Kaye movies over and over again. He never minded bringing Mary Lee and me to the corner drugstore, where we sat at the marble soda fountain, devoured coffee ice cream, and read comic books.

My mother had to keep a close eye on him because he was so absent-minded. He once took me to the movies without any underpants. Another time, he brought me home without my shoes. When I went out with him, my mother would caution me, "Hold onto his jacket." She was afraid he would forget I was with him and walk off without me.

My father operated an ongoing crap game for the employees of the Barnum and Bailey Circus. This enterprise was known as the G Tent (G for Gambling) and made him a decent living for twenty-five years. He brought me a framed picture of the famous Gargantua, a huge, ferocious gorilla, supposedly scarred when a handler hurled acid in his face. I sat in the front row when the circus came to town—and Emmett Kelly, that sad, wonderful clown, swept his little spot-light over to where I sat and looked at me with his forlorn eyes.

"Ma*dame*," my father would say, "When the kid grows up, we'll put her in the circus. If she stays this size, we'll put her in with the midgets. If she grows, she can be a giant." Then he would sit down on the sofa, still wearing his hat—light up a cigar and read the *Daily News*. My father was only kidding about putting me in the circus—but looking back on it now—I think I was already there.

DADDY'S TEMPER WAS FEROCIOUS. I would hear him on the phone shouting at his partner, "the Greek." He said when you had a Greek for a friend, you didn't need an enemy. My parents' arguments were frightening. Sometimes I would wake in the middle of the night to my mother's hysterical yelling. "She's my daughter and she's staying here with me from now on," she would scream. "Stop torturing me about it. She's not going!"

She'd later say, "Your father tortured me every year to send you down there."

Torture. That was my mother's favorite word. It was hard to tell, from my vantage point, who was torturing whom.

I absorbed a lot of information about the world I was living in from my father. He had this great way of telling a story. Sometimes, he'd lapse into Pig Latin just for a laugh. "Ixnay on the ackencray," he'd say. He did card tricks. He enjoyed telling my mother she'd better shape up, *or else*.

"One day, Madame, you're gonna open the door and Tough Tony or Killer Kane'll be standin' there."

I have no doubt that, somewhere out there, there *really was* a Killer Kane and a Tough Tony. Of course, they weren't coming to see my mother. But Daddy thought it was very funny to mention them on a regular basis.

He told me about somebody called "Sleep-out Louie." "Sleep-out never wanted to leave the crap game, so he'd lay on a cot in the back room, take a little nap, and then jump back in the game. That way, he could play for days and not miss anything. That's why they called him 'Sleep-out.'"

My father had a million stories. I liked to hear him tell about the time, before the war, some German Jews came to New York in search of a hit man to assassinate Hitler. Some jokester steered them to my father where he was living at the Piccadilly Hotel. He set up a meeting with them in the Piccadilly Drugstore to discuss the situation.

"See that guy over there?" my father said, pointing to someone handpicked for his ferocious looks, seated conspicuously at the far end of the soda fountain. "That guy has killed *seventeen* men."

The Jewish businessmen were suitably impressed. They didn't know that my father, with all the skills of a casting agent, had rounded up a collection of the toughest-looking hooligans he could find, complete with prominent scars or broken noses. Nary a killer among them.

They gave my father the contract to sail over to Germany and get the job done. He and a few pals booked passage—and presently arrived in Berlin. There they remained, wining and dining themselves, without the slightest intention of assassinating anyone. Periodically, they sent telegrams to their benefactors. "Attempt failed. Stop. Send money. Stop."

Eventually, these messages began to lose the ring of truth. The jig was up and Banjo and his cohorts packed their bags and returned home.

It never occurred to my father to feel guilty about taking money from these naïve Europeans who were trying to divert the disaster that they could see coming. He figured that *nobody* could get to Hitler—and if *he* didn't take the money from these suckers—*somebody else would.*

Louie Levine, Carole & Banjo

DADDY CALLED ME *"THE MEAL-TICKET."* He would often tell my mother, "Don't worry, Madame. As long as you have the meal-ticket, you'll always be taken care of." I was his insurance policy. I think his words were a testament to the esteem that my father felt for his brother-in-law. He took solace in his belief that if, for any reason, he couldn't take care of his wife and child, his brother-in-law always would.

In that belief, he was correct.

UNCLE JIM WOULDN'T HURT A FLY—

OR WOULD HE?

B y 1950 gambling was all washed up in Florida. Gone were the days when a slot machine could be found in every drugstore. Gone were the glamorous evenings at the Colonial Inn, the Boheme, and the Greenacres. Gone, the excitement of the gaming rooms, the stars, the café society clientele, women with ankle-length gowns and upswept hair, men in dark suits or sporty jackets—a time when every day was New Year's Eve. The Colonial Inn was the last to go.

One of the major reasons for the death of the illegal but delightful gaming business in South Florida was the emergence of Senator Estes Kefauver. In the late Forties, Senator Kefauver, who would later go on to make a bid for the presidency, was gearing up to create a name for himself using the time-honored method of investigating Organized Crime. He went from state to state (while avoiding his home state of Tennessee) targeting, for the most part, such "heinous" crimes as gambling and bookmaking. (Years later, ethical considerations aside, gambling would be taken up by the United States Government in the form of OTBs).

In Broward County, he hit the mother lode. Sheriff Walter Clark was called before the committee and raked over the coals for his support of wide-open gambling, while he gamely protested that gambling, "helped the economy."

"I didn't think it was my job to close casinos," he said.

Kefauver quietly, but firmly stated, "Hallandale Beach is the sin capital of the South. A wide open den of iniquity."

Meyer appeared before the Kefauver Committee and admitted that he knew Joe Adonis, Frank Costello, Lucky Luciano, and Vincent Alo. Although, for a little man, he had a surprisingly deep voice, he managed to look and sound like a mild-mannered accountant. To most of the committee's questions, he pled the Fifth. He would be called several times and would consistently refer to his constitutional right to refuse to incriminate himself.

Frank Costello, with his gravelly voice, appeared before the committee every day for a week. Virginia Hill (consort of the late Bugsy Seigel) in her fur stole and picture hat, provided plenty of excitement as she abused reporters, shouting and kicking her way out of the committee room. Years later, in Europe, she would commit suicide.

Television discovered the entertainment value of the crime committee, and it seemed that all of America was watching. In March of 1951, Kefauver's face appeared on the cover of *Time Magazine*, bearing witness to the riveting impression he had made on a nation that couldn't seem to get enough of "cops and robbers."

Forty years later, Uncle Jim would reminisce: "We couldn't wait to sell off all that land. The beachfront property of the Boheme alone, down there at the end of Hallandale Beach Boulevard, would have been worth a fortune if we had waited. But what did we know? We were dummies."

ON MONROE STREET, life went on as usual. My uncle and aunt played golf every day. Their friends visited the house with regularity. We still went out as a family on Thursdays and Sundays; but instead of the clubs, we frequented certain favored restaurants. We'd sit at long tables with Uncle Jim's pals and their wives, while waiters hovered around. My favorite place was Jimmy DeFeo's on the 79th Street Causeway in Miami. Just by coincidence, DeFeo happened to be a cousin of my father's. He and his wife lived in a house behind the restaurant; and after I ate, I could go next door and play with his daughter while the grown-ups lingered over coffee and dessert. Wherever we went, Uncle Jim got the royal treatment.

Jimmy golfing

At home, dinner was served promptly at 5:30, with Uncle Jim at one end of the table and Aunty Doe at the other. The rest of us filled in at the sides. There was me. There was my mother a great deal of the time. There was my grandfather, Harry, who lived at the house since my grandmother had passed away. Harry was a crotchety old geezer who rarely spoke. When he wasn't fishing, he spent most of his time sitting in front of the house with Duke, the brown Doberman Pincer Uncle Jim had been given by Bill Syms, the owner of the Hollywood Dog Track. Uncle Jim and Auntie Doe weren't exactly animal lovers. They considered Duke a watchdog and he was never allowed in the house.

I was dying to have a horse, like the two Kovalick girls, Judy and Phyllis, who lived around the corner. I spent a lot of time at their house. Their father, Phil, a beefy, tough-looking man, would often stop in at our house and sit in the kitchen with a cigar and a cup of coffee.

Years later, I would discover that Phil Kovalick was once described by Damon Runyon in his syndicated column, The Brighter Side, as a "glowering, heavy-set chap" often known by his Yiddish name of Farvel. Runyon told the story of how Farvel, along with two female companions, was turned away from the Stork Club one night in 1945—and how he warned the Stork Club's owner, Sherman Billingsley that he would, "show you how we handle such things." Several months later, two men in blue overcoats ran through the front door and hurled a couple of stink bombs into the club's vestibule. Billingsley was able to identify a picture of Farvel as one of the two men, but declined to pursue the matter.

Phil Kovalick would one day be murdered and found sealed in a steel drum floating in the Intercoastal Waterway.

I NEVER GOT over wanting a horse and I never got one. My uncle had been known to horseback ride in Hot Springs, Arkansas, during the Thirties—but by this time, I think the only horses he was conscious of were the ones that ran at the racetrack. Pet horses, along with boats and swimming pools, were luxuries Uncle Jim found unnecessary.

A regular at our dinner table was Niggy Flax. Niggy was short, swarthy, and had kinky hair and a large Durante-style nose. He always sat to the right of Uncle Jim, taking the role of court jester. He was a bookmaker and every day he would sadly lament about this or that horse race that didn't go his way. What bet he should or shouldn't have taken. Niggy made Uncle Jim laugh. Sometimes, Uncle Jim would make *us* laugh, like when he told how he was once known as "Swivel-hips Jimmy." He claimed he got the name because he was such a great football player. I'm pretty sure he was kidding.

God help any fly that snuck through a screen door at dinner time. Uncle Jim was the sworn enemy of flies. He would attack them viciously with a rolled-up newspaper and not give up until he triumphed.

Hattie was still the queen of the kitchen where she hummed softly as she whipped up delicious meals of lamb stew or fried chicken and made the best apple pie in the world. She always had a helper to do the heavy housecleaning and serve dinner. Aunty Doe would ring a little silver bell when it was time for the table to be cleared.

The television would be on in the sunroom, adjacent to the dining room—so that we could hear the news of the day. Politics was often discussed at the table, with Uncle Jim dominating the conversation. When the Kefauver Committee was being televised, Uncle Jim scrutinized the screen, muttering about " . . . this no good rat-bastard, Kefauver."

AFTER THE CAROLE RITA BEAUTY SALON closed in New York, my mother changed her routine. Instead of several trips a year, she came to Florida more-or-less permanently. Uncle Jim got her a job as a telephone operator at one of the Miami Beach Hotels and she moved into my room, bag, baggage, and dog. So I had a roommate.

My father would come down every so often and always stayed at the old Great Southern Hotel on Hollywood Boulevard. My mother couldn't wait for him to leave.

My mother was the only member of the family who attended Mass and when she and I were together, in either Florida or New York, she took me. Uncle Jim had no use for religion and Aunty Doe didn't seem concerned about it, either. What I didn't understand, at the time, was that my aunt was out of favor with the Church because of her divorce. I guess that put her in a bad position, so she just gave up on it. My mother had an early divorce in her distant past, too; but she didn't seem to be losing any sleep over it.

My aunt saw to it that I made my First Communion, which turned out to be a traumatic experience because of the grouchy old priest who yelled at me for speaking too softly in the confessional when I recited my "sins." When the time came for me to make my Confirmation, I dug my heels in and said, "No!" By the time I reached puberty, I had decided that the whole religion thing, as it had been presented to me, made no sense. I would be an atheist, like Uncle Jim.

I shared an intimacy with my mother that didn't exist with my aunt. My mother and I laughed and talked like friends. Daddy came and went. He cooked his own meals. He was like an afterthought. My mother explained to me that he was much older than her—and that she had married him out of a need to be taken care of.

In my uncle and aunt's house, there was a sense of formality. They both gave off an air of authority: he, over everyone—she, over everyone but him. As I got older and issues of discipline arose, tensions developed between my mother and my aunt. One evening, in Florida, I came to the dinner table wearing lipstick. My aunt told me to go and wash it off.

"She doesn't have to," my mother said. "She's *my* daughter and don't you forget it."

"If she's your daughter then why don't you spend a little more time with her?" my aunt snapped.

Just before I stalked off dramatically to my room, I glanced at Uncle Jim who sat at the end of the table calmly chewing each bite one hundred times.

My usually taciturn grandfather chimed in, "Why don't you give her the back of your hand, Flo?"

My mother told him to mind his own business.

"All right!" Uncle Jim declared. "Let's keep it down to a roar!" Which was his way of telling everyone to shut the hell up.

Not long after that my father came to Florida, showed up at the house in a rage, and created a scene. He was waving a note, (He called it a *"red-hot love letter"*) that he had somehow gotten a-hold of. The note was to my mother from a French chef who worked at a Miami Beach hotel with her. Amidst the shouting, it became abundantly clear to me why she had been taking French lessons and madly doing daily exercises. I was twelve and beginning to wonder why my mother didn't put an end to this mess of a marriage.

HAVANA

In 1953, President Truman completed his eight years. Uncle Jim said Truman was a son-of-a-bitch and good riddance. Eisenhower took over and looked like everybody's favorite grandpa; but, according to Uncle Jim, "Politicians are bloodsuckers who feed off the people."

Uncle Jim was a rugged individualist who didn't have much use for the government or any type of authority. The FBI was always parked up the street, but he ignored them. One Sunday, an FBI agent had the nerve to come to the kitchen door. He asked Uncle Jim if he could come in for a cup of coffee. Uncle Jim just laughed.

"Is this what you went to four years of college for?" he asked, "to follow a guy like me around?"

I understood that our phones were tapped and that I was never to talk on the phone about spending money, but I didn't give any of that much thought since I was too busy figuring out what my fashion style should be and working on developing a really good walk. I wore Uncle Jim's big white shirts over my blue jeans and I rashly took a scissors and cut my hair short, the way Liz Taylor was wearing hers. My aunt went to the beauty shop twice a week, but you wouldn't catch me dead in one of those places.

My mother had convinced my aunt (courtesy of Uncle Jim's money) to invest in yet another business venture. It was the same deal as the Carole Rita Beauty Salon. In my mother's dress shop, she was the working partner. The shop was on Harrison Street, a block south of Hollywood Boulevard. My mother was always trying to make a go of something and was very happy running her own little business.

I think my mother found it hard to be overshadowed by her sister.

"Flo is a beauty," people said. "Flo's taste is impeccable. She always looks like she just stepped out of a band box."

Every so often, Aunty Doe would give my mother a stack of her very expensive dresses. My mother would pass them on to one of her friends. She resented being given her sister's hand-me-downs. And, besides, she didn't need them.

Jimmy & Flo with Flo's sons, Billy & Larry Miller

Aunty Doe disapproved of my mother's life-style. She complained to Uncle Jim that my mother frequently went out at night.

"For Christ's sake, Grace, why don't you stay home, once in a while, and help Carole with her homework," she would say to my mother.

"Why the hell should the two of us sit home with her, when you're here anyway?"

It would be a shouting match until Uncle Jim came in the room and repeated his usual, "Keep it down to a roar."

Aunty Doe's temper could erupt at any moment. A spilt glass of milk at the dinner table could bring on a tirade. She and I often clashed. She didn't like my hair, my clothes, or my attitude. One of my favorite moves was to storm into my bedroom and slam the door as hard as I could, locking it behind me. Then, after sweeping everything off my dresser onto the floor and kicking a few pieces of furniture, I would lounge on my bed with a book in my lap, pretending to read. This was especially satisfying, as my aunt beat on the door, screaming she was going to break my neck when she got her hands on me.

My new "fuck you" attitude earned me a dismissal from the Pine Crest School, where I had gone for the past five years. We went up to Fort Lauderdale to have a showdown with the principal, Mrs. MacMillan. Though my aunt tried her best to change Mrs. MacMillan's mind about expelling me, it was a no-go.

Adding insult to injury, Mrs. MacMillan, a tightly corseted matron, noted that perhaps my "background" had something to do with my bad behavior. That remark must have really needled my aunt. We left in silent disgrace and I finished out the year in a funky little private school in Hollywood.

My mother held my aunt responsible for my troubles at Pine Crest. She would say to me in private, "Your uncle and aunt stole you, you know."

The atmosphere around the house was chilly, punctuated by occasional eruptions when my aunt and mother could no longer keep their emotions in check. Sweet-natured Frannie, Cousin Larry's wife, was there one night, during one of these blowouts. She was shocked when she saw my aunt knock my mother down the three steps that led into the sunken living room.

I spent as much time as I could at Frannie's house. She was lonely because Larry was working over in Havana, where Uncle Jim had gotten him a job in the casino at the Hotel Nacional de Cuba. Frannie, a tall, slender redhead who hailed from Texas, was a dancer and had worked in the production shows at the Colonial Inn. We would often have a ballet class in her sunroom after which she would make juicy and delicious tomato sandwiches. She gave me *The Complete Works of Shakespeare* that year for Christmas. She was always there to lend a sympathetic ear. I loved her and felt that she was a kindred spirit.

Cousin Larry's wife, Frannie

I FOUND myself in a spiral of depression. My somber behavior and outbursts of temper were met head-on by my aunt, but even her staunch efforts couldn't thwart my stubborn resolve to have my own way.

One day, there was a nasty scene between my aunt and me when she discovered I had invited some boys into the house to raid the liquor cabinet. Uncle Jim usually left such matters to the women. He was a man's man and didn't want to deal with all that emotion.

This time, however, he decided to get involved.

He came into my bedroom. Adopting his characteristic macho stance, weight on one leg, hands on hips, he glared at me. "What the hell's the matter with you?"

I tried to explain to him about my anger and my feelings of abandonment.

"Why didn't my mother want me?" I cried.

"Now look," he reasoned. "Your mother was busy with other things and we thought it would be better for you to live with us. What's wrong with that?"

"You don't understand," I wailed.

"You just need to change your attitude," he told me.

Looking into his eyes, it was clear that I would never get through to him.

Just change your attitude, he had said. To him, everything was black and white. If everybody just did things his way, everything would turn out okay. I could feel my sense of isolation increasing with every breath I took. I was an outcast. I didn't belong anywhere. I was sick of them all.

MY AUNT WENT to my mother's dress shop and told my mother, "Grace, I'd like to look over the books, if you don't mind."

"Well, I do mind," my mother answered.

Before you knew it, they were grappling with each other and pretty much managed to wreck the store.

My mother grabbed the phone and called the police station; but when the officer arrived, he turned out to be Cousin Billy's best friend, Eddie Dickerman.

My mother wanted to press charges; but Eddie said, "Come on now, Gracie, you don't really want to do that, do you?"

So my mother gave in and the whole thing was dropped. But that was the end of their partnership. It was the end of their relationship too—what was left of it.

My mother rented one of those old Thirties Florida cottages on the wrong side of town, and I felt it was my duty to go with her. Besides, by that time, I didn't like my aunt very much. She was uptight about boys and things like what I was wearing. When I bleached the front of my hair blond, she had a fit. She said my clothes were too tight and I should wear a *girdle*, for God's sake. She was really cramping my style and I wanted to get away from her. But once I was out of the Monroe Street house and into this tattered little bungalow with my mother, I felt more displaced than ever. I listened to a lot of Billie Holiday, which corresponded to my blue mood.

I still spent plenty of time at my uncle and aunt's house, and often ate dinner there. For a while, Joe Adonis's daughter, Maria, who was in Florida to attend college, temporarily occupied my room. Maria was vivacious and funny. I would sit with her in the evening and watch as she applied her make-up—a time-consuming process that fascinated me. She was glamorous and reminded me of the Italian movie star, Gina Lollabrigida.

I was at the house, one afternoon when Meyer's daughter, Sandra, looking preppy in Bermuda shorts and knee socks, came over to speak to Uncle Jim. She was sixteen and unhappy at home. She and Meyer's wife, Teddy, didn't get along; and Sandra wanted her father's permission to get married. Uncle Jim thought she might as well, even though the man she had in mind was a lot older than she was. Uncle Jim weighed in on the side of letting her get married. "Let her do whatever she wants," he told Meyer. "What's the use of fighting it?"

AFTER KEFAUVER PUT an end to gambling in Florida, Meyer Lansky turned his full attention toward Cuba. Although Meyer, Uncle Jim, and their other partners had an interest in the Flamingo and the Desert Inn in Las Vegas, Cuba was closer to home. They could operate freely there, which they couldn't do anywhere in the United States because of their notoriety. If Kefauver killed the goose that laid the golden egg in Florida—well, they would just pick themselves up and go where they were wanted—and where they could do what they did better than anybody else.

Dating back to the Forties, Meyer had forged a strong relationship with the Cuban leader, Fulgencio Batista. Because of that, he was able to secure a lease which enabled him to create a gambling concession in the beautiful, old Hotel Nacional de Cuba.

A few years later construction would begin on what Meyer considered his crowning achievement: the Riviera Hotel, twenty-one stories high, overlooking the iconic promenade called the Malecon that stretches along Havana's coast. It would be the largest casino-hotel anywhere in the world at that time, with the exception of Las Vegas.

Fulgencio Batista encouraged Meyer's presence in Cuba because his government was intent on promoting tourism. He knew that gambling—especially the honest, high-class version of it that was Meyer's trademark—would be advantageous for the Cuban economy.

IN SPITE of the frequent flare-ups between my mother and my aunt about how I should be raised, Uncle Jim remained his usual, unflappable self. Every morning he came down the winding staircase in his terry robe and leather slippers to have his breakfast of toasted roll, orange juice, and coffee—and to read the morning papers in the recently redecorated pink and gray kitchen. He seemed to reside in a sea of composure.

Auntie Doe, on the other hand, seemed to have dried up from within. The necessary restrictions of a gall-bladder diet had caused her to lose weight. And due to the battle between her and my mother, a heavy load descended upon her and squeezed out the last bit of lightness and gaiety she possessed.

AT THE END of the school year in June of 1954, Uncle Jim surprised Aunty Doe and me by announcing, "We're taking a trip to Cuba."

We flew over in a small plane and were met at the airport by Dino Cellini, who was in charge of running the casino at the Hotel Nacional de Cuba where we would be staying. Dino was a handsome man in his thirties and I secretly developed a mad crush on him—which made it a little difficult to concentrate as he showed us the sights of Havana.

Our rooms in the hotel had tall French windows overlooking the gardens below. White gauze hung from canopies above the mahogany beds to protect from marauding mosquitoes.

Dino wined and dined us and gave us a daily tour of the city. We saw exquisite European architecture, walked from palm-shaded sidewalks into luxurious shops, drove through narrow streets past crumbling cemeteries.

We went to see the show at Tropicana, the famous nightclub that featured an outrageous open-air floor show exploding with Latin rhythms and showgirls, feathered and bejeweled, who really knew how to shake their maracas. It was like the old days of the Colonial Inn on steroids. Under the stars, Uncle Jim rumbaed smoothly around the dance floor—with both Aunty Doe and me.

We ended our trip with a visit to Veradero Beach, where we spent several days swimming and relaxing at a quiet oceanfront hotel. My uncle and aunt were decidedly middle-aged, while I was headed toward a turbulent adolescence.

BAD DAUGHTER

After the Cuba trip, Uncle Jim and Auntie Doe packed up and returned to New York for the summer. My mother and I stayed in Florida through the stifling heat as she struggled to keep the dress shop afloat. Finally, my mother closed the store for the rest of the summer and we boarded a train and headed north. No cozy compartment like the old days traveling with my aunt. Just an uncomfortable chair to spend the night on, sleeping amidst the little old ladies with their egg sandwiches.

Once we reached New York, though, I couldn't have been happier. It was mostly just me and my mother in the apartment, because my father came and went. Sometimes to Saratoga for the races. Sometimes off somewhere with the circus. My mother's friend, Jeanne Hutchinson, would visit in the evening and bring peach ice cream, which we ate on the balcony, looking out over the treetops of Central Park. Jeanne had a gentle quality that was doubly interesting to me since I knew that she was an atheist, like Uncle Jim. This confirmed for me the notion that church attendance wasn't necessarily a requirement for achieving goodness.

Mary Lee Dearring and her mother, Lee, were a constant in our New York life. I loved hanging out in Mary Lee's dressing room at the Broadhurst Theatre, where she was appearing on Broadway in the hit comedy, *Anniversary Waltz*. I watched in fascination the frantic backstage activity as actors and technicians ran through their paces. I envied Mary Lee's life as an actor. In my heart, it was what I wished for myself.

In the fall, I was back in Florida where, as Uncle Jim had predicted, my bad attitude had finally gotten me kicked out of Pine Crest. I was sent to the scrubby, ugly public high school in Hollywood, which was a culture shock. All too quickly, I made the acquaintance of the fast, "in" crowd. Liquor, sex, and teen-age drama were rampant; and soon, I was getting drunk at parties along with my newfound friends. I wore dark glasses at all times and sandals laced up the leg, the way I had seen them worn in Greenwich Village. When sufficiently drunk, I was prone to recite poetry or sing jazz.

I saw *Rebel without a Cause* at least ten times—lost in my own angst as I drank in James Dean's tortured, sensitive face and shared every painful moment he endured. When I heard the news of his death, I cried all day.

I was fourteen and out of control. I got in bed with my clothes on in order to climb out the window as soon as my mother was asleep. I rode around in cars all night long, drinking beer and sleeping with my head on the desk the next day at school.

My mother whined and complained about me to anyone who would listen—but she couldn't cope with me or protect me from myself. It felt like no one was in charge of the ship. That's when I started thinking it might be best to move back with my uncle and aunt.

Carole, age 14

I MET Bill Stephens on a blind date. He was handsome, with dark brown hair and slanted turquoise eyes. He was wearing a pink oxford shirt and white cotton pants that were rolled up slightly; and I noticed that he wore white sneakers without socks. He spoke in a deep melodious voice. And to top it all off . . . he was smoking a pipe.

This was like nothing I had seen before. The boys I knew wore blue jeans and tee shirts. They didn't wear pink shirts and they certainly didn't smoke pipes! I was completely awestruck by his air of sophistication.

From the moment I met him, Bill consumed my every waking hour. He drove me to school in the morning and picked me up each afternoon. I wanted to move back with my uncle and aunt, so one afternoon, we piled all my things into his car and I returned to Monroe Street. My mother never forgave him for helping me move. She would later say that I was a "bad daughter" because I had "abandoned" her. How ironic that she never realized it was *she* who had abandoned *me*. She was expert at placing blame anywhere but on herself.

My uncle and aunt were happy to have me back. In spite of the fact that, at nineteen, he was five years older than I was—they didn't have any major objections to Bill. He was charming, friendly—very much a contrast to my sullen disposition. He lightened the atmosphere.

Bill was an artist and an intellectual. I was drawn to him because he opened up a world to me that differed deeply from the world I had been born into. He introduced me to the beautiful world of Picasso, Sartre, Frank Lloyd Wright. He painted me. We read poetry together.

When Bill heard that Billie Holiday was appearing at a raunchy Miami nightclub called the Ball and Chain, he brought me there. I'll never forget the sadness I felt seeing her in that shabby place. Though I knew of her struggles with drugs, I was shocked when I saw her haggard face and swollen ankles. She stood in a pool of light, stared straight ahead, and seemed to will herself to sing.

Bill's parents showed up at the house and introduced themselves to my uncle and aunt. This probably took a lot of moxie on their part, since my uncle's reputation preceded him and they surely knew who he was.

Mr. Stephens, a high-strung sales executive with *Esquire Magazine*, looked like W.C. Fields and loped around the living room, one hand shoved in his pocket, tensely jingling coins together like Captain Queeg.

Mrs. Stephens, a tall, attractive Norwegian, kept oddly silent, except for an occasional nervous laugh that sounded something like a whooping cough.

Bill and I watched from the next room as Uncle Jim eyed Mr. Stephens dubiously.

Finally, Mr. Stephens spoke. "Carole and Bill are awfully young to be seeing so much of each other, don't you think, Jim?"

Uncle Jim was silent as he shifted his ever-present toothpick in his mouth. His eyes became slits. "Why? Is there something I should be worried about?"

"Oh, *nooo*, Jim! Absolutely not! Nothing to worry about," Mr. Stephens assured him.

Uncle Jim nodded slowly, not entirely convinced.

BILL and I continued to see each other every day. My aunt and uncle's antennae were up, but they took a wait and see attitude. They didn't have to wait long.

A few months into the relationship, my aunt came into my room.

"Are you in trouble?" she asked.

Aunty Doe wasted no time. She called a friend of hers who knew just how to take care of such things. The next morning, I was whisked away by my aunt's friend to a run-down Miami clinic, where a sleazy doctor terminated the pregnancy. When I arrived home, I walked past Uncle Jim who was sitting in the kitchen, and went directly to my bedroom. I awoke in the middle of the night covered in blood and managed to climb to the upstairs bedroom. Uncle Jim was conspicuously absent. I screamed at my aunt to take me to the hospital, but she said she couldn't do that; and I spent a terrifying night hemorrhaging, not knowing whether I was going to live or die.

Abortions were illegal in those days so my aunt faced a tough decision. I'm sure that Uncle Jim's identity was uppermost in her mind. She took a big risk that night. I can only wonder what I would have done in her place.

If I had been sullen before—after that I was enraged. Although I was relieved to be rid of the problem, I felt no gratitude towards my aunt. I refused to go to school. I stayed in my room and barely spoke. Bill's parents came to the house to confer with my uncle and aunt. I wanted nothing to do with Bill. As a result, he suffered a breakdown and was sent to the Yale Psychiatric Institute in New Haven, Connecticut.

All of this brought about the abrupt end of my formal education. No amount of persuasion or coercion could make me go back to school. My aunt, for her part, just wanted to get the hell out of Florida.

Uncle Jim had told me several months before this that I suffered from "a bad attitude." Now, however, he had nothing to say to me.

These were women's issues. Besides, it would have been unthinkable, in our family, for such things to be discussed. It was the mid-fifties, so I don't think we were unique in that regard.

We just packed up, left it all behind us—and headed for New York.

BLACK SHEEP

Manhattan was a bazaar that offered everything my fourteen-year-old heart craved. It was liberating to escape from Florida and the teenage misery it represented.

Although I had visited my uncle and aunt's Riverside Drive apartment since I was a toddler, crouching under the grand piano, it was the first time I had actually lived there. Now, my severance from my mother was complete. While she stayed permanently in Florida, my father maintained the Central Park West apartment and continued in his usual vagabond ways.

Uncle Jim's study became my bedroom. It was loaded with books, and framed, softly-tinted pictures of racehorses and jockeys adorned the walls. The room became my sanctuary.

We had no Hattie in New York—and Aunty Doe didn't cook—so we ate out every night. There were certain restaurants that Uncle Jim preferred. Frankie & Johnny's was an old speakeasy up a rickety staircase on West Forty-Sixth Street. There we ate thick steaks, lamb chops, chopped salad with anchovies, creamed spinach, and liver with onions. Around the corner, Dinty Moore's was a slice of the past dating back to pre-Prohibition days. It had black and white floors, brass railings and autographed eight-by-tens lining the walls.

Unlike today, when your New York waiter is likely to be an out-of-work actor who introduces himself and sits down at the table to take your order, the waiters in these places were professionals—old men wearing bow ties and white aprons, moving quickly on long-suffering feet to serve steaming dishes of potted chicken or beef brisket.

There was always a celebrity or two in view and Uncle Jim seemed to know them all, from J. Edgar Hoover to Mike Todd. One evening, as we walked into Moore's, Aunty Doe spotted the widely disliked columnist, Lee Mortimer, seated alone in a corner.

"Oh," she quipped, "There's Lee Mortimer...having dinner with all his friends."

Uncle Jim always had an entourage and at that time there was a cast of seven or eight regulars. There was Doc Rosen, a dentist, and his wife, Roz, who lived a few blocks from my parents, in the Century Apartments. We all had our teeth attended to (cavities filled minus Novocaine) at his office, which was on the ground floor of my parents' building.

Henrí Giné, an elegant man who hailed from the lower East Side, was with Music Corporation of America, an important theatrical agency. He and his wife, Billie, had been a dance team, but Henrí became an agent after suffering a broken back in a freak accident. Henri worked for Frank Sinatra and he and Billie were very close to Sinatra's parents, Dolly and Marty.

Babe and Edna Mann were an elderly couple who were fun, in spite of the fact that they seemed ancient to me. I never knew what Babe's story was, but he was like a gentle, perpetually smiling marionette. Edna had been the type of singer rudely known, back in the day, as a "coon-shouter." She was a pint-sized, sprightly old bird who could be counted on to break into song at any given moment. Many years later, I was incredulous to read somewhere that Edna was a "bag-lady," employed to transport skimmed money from Las Vegas casinos. Really?

Last but certainly not least of my uncle's happy little gang was George Wood. George was one of the major players at the William Morris Theatrical Agency. He was known as the agency troubleshooter and handled the most difficult stars, such as Sinatra. He and Uncle Jim had been close pals for many years, and he had been responsible for providing the star power for the Colonial Inn during its brief shining existence.

Flo & Jimmy, Edna & Babe Mann, Roz & Doc Rosen , Billie & Henri Gine, Niggie Flax

As always, Uncle Jim's life was calm and orderly. A light breakfast as he read the papers, then he'd be off to get a shave. I had no idea where he went or what he did every day—nor did it ever occur to me to wonder about it.

Aunty Doe went to the beauty shop twice a week to maintain her hair and nails. We dressed for dinner. They no longer went to the theater as they once had. They had reached the age where it was common for them to attend funerals.

On Sundays, Uncle Jim would spend the day with his brother, Doctor Joe. Aunty Doe and I would usually stay at home and order in from the Chinese restaurant next door. I realize now that my aunt disliked both Uncle Jim's mother and his sister-in-law—and just refused to go. There were a lot of people my aunt didn't care much for, but had to tolerate, because of Uncle Jim. She evidently didn't feel that necessity applied to her in-laws.

When we did accompany him, Uncle Jim would hire a driver who would take us through the Bronx and into the suburb of Westchester. There, we would arrive at a large brick house nestled in a rustic setting, which was the home of my uncle's younger brother, the affable Dr. Joe. A taller and even more soft-spoken version of his brother, he had the bumbling personality of an Ed Wynn. He had gone to medical school in Italy (financed by Uncle Jim), and it was there that he met his wife, Lena.

Also present at these family gatherings was my uncle's widowed mother who spoke no English and his spinster sister, Lizzie, who had spent her whole life caring for and being controlled by her domineering mother. It was always a tense day.

"Mina son," the old lady would murmur, staring at Uncle Jim.

Uncle Jim would switch the toothpick from one side of his mouth to the other and nod his head lightly.

Lena always kept up a nervous chatter, which was a good thing, because Aunty Doe contributed nothing but stony silence.

Even though his mother seemed to make a fuss over her eldest son, the underlying truth was that, no matter how much money he made or how much he helped his family, in her eyes, Uncle Jim was a gangster and would never overcome his "disgrace." I'm guessing that my aunt never forgave the old lady for that.

The late summer of 1956 found Uncle Jim scrutinizing the Democratic National Convention in Chicago. The black and white eye of the TV blinked away as the Democratic Party nominated Adlai Stevenson for president, over the old nemesis, Estes Kefauver. Uncle Jim couldn't have been happier.

Kefauver narrowly beat out the relatively unknown John F. Kennedy for the democratic vice-presidential nomination. When the Eisenhower/Nixon ticket easily defeated Stevenson and his running mate, Kefauver—once again, Uncle Jim was delighted.

He didn't foresee the emergence of John Kennedy on the national scene, nor did he suspect that Kennedy's race for the presidency would pull him into its vortex. Uncle Jim could not foresee then how Kennedy's advancing ascendancy would affect his own future.

As soon as I arrived in New York, my passion for dance returned and Uncle Jim was more than happy to finance my studies.

My days began with an apple for breakfast, then rushing off to dance class at Carnegie Hall where I took three, four, five classes a day. On weekends, Mary Lee and I took to wandering around Greenwich Village. If New York was heaven—then the Village was Nirvana. I don't know if Mary Lee had previously had much interest in the area. Maybe to her, it was just the neighborhood she happened to live in. But I couldn't get enough of it. The Beatniks of the Village mirrored all the rebelliousness and dissatisfaction with the status quo that I was experiencing within myself. I felt right at home.

Walking down MacDougal Street with its silversmiths, sandal-makers, bookshops, and coffee houses was like being at a carnival midway. You could stop in at the Figaro to sip a cappuccino at a marble-topped table and watch the sandaled avant-garde stroll by —the longhaired boys, the hairy-legged girls. On Sundays, folk singers gathered with their guitars and banjos in the dry fountain in Washington Square Park, while old men played chess under the trees. The singing would go on for hours and everybody would join in to sing songs like "John Henry" and "The Rock Island Line."

One spring evening, while Mary Lee and I lay on the grass amid hundreds of others, breathing in the acrid smell of weed while listening to chamber music, Eddie Lewis came along all dressed in white and charmed himself into our company. He was slender with a fawn-like beauty and his skin was the color of coffee laced with milk. From that night on, I couldn't stop thinking about him.

I was very clever at finding ways to be with him and Mary Lee became my willing accomplice. Eddie and I spent most of our time walking around the city hand in hand.

One night, Eddie and I went to listen to jazz and drink Sloe Gin Fizzes and I got drunk enough to cut myself free from all restraint. I wasn't ever going home. I spent the night with Eddie and the next evening we took the subway up to Central Park to hear Billie Holiday sing. In the open-air amphitheater under the stars, I saw her for the second and last time, for she was soon to die. Because Eddie's roommate was a jazz musician and knew one of her sidemen, we were able to go backstage after the concert.

There was the great Lady Day, resting on a chair, her hair pulled back tightly from her ashen face. Brief introductions were made. She mumbled softly. I'm sure I didn't say a thing. Her weary eyes, ancient as the night sky, looked through us. Did I shake her hand? Memory fails me.

I was still soaring from this mind-blowing experience as we climbed the stone steps leading up to the west side of the park. Just then, one of Uncle Jim's perennial dinner companions, Doc Rosen, spotted me in the crowd.

He grabbed my arm and pulled me aside. "Carole, what the hell do you think you're doing?" he hissed. "Do you realize your aunt is in the hospital with a nervous collapse because of you?"

"That's her problem," I said, my voice dripping with teen-age spitefulness. "I'm not going back."

"Well," he said, eyeing my friends in disgust, "the least you can do is have the decency to go home and talk to your uncle."

I answered him with a snotty, "Sure, why not? I need to pick up a few of my things anyway."

With a quick, "I'll see you later," to Eddie, I returned with Doc to Riverside Drive.

I was nervous and didn't know what to expect, but I decided to fake it. "I just came back to get a few things," I told my uncle.

"That's what you think," he answered.

"I'm going to leave and you can't stop me," I yelled.

Uncle Jim was a man of few words but he was a man of action. He locked the front door and sat down on the couch. Recognizing that he was immovable, I did the only thing I could do. I retreated to my room, got into bed, and fell into a fitful sleep.

The next day, Uncle Jim took me to the hospital. My aunt was lying limply on the bed. Henrí and Billie Giné stood silently against the wall. Saying that I needed to use the rest room, I went to a pay phone to ring Eddie's number. When he answered, I could hear a lot of shouting going on in the background. I realized immediately that my uncle had sent somebody to warn Eddie and his friends to stay away from me.

Infuriated, I barreled back into my aunt's room like gangbusters, boiling with rage. How dare they pull these strong-arm tactics and interfere in my life like that? Aunty Doe started to say something about how rotten I was, how thoughtless, how my mother would have her head on a platter if anything should ever happen to me.

I screamed out, "I hate you all! I'm leaving and there's nothing you can fucking do about it!"

I grabbed a vase full of flowers and hurled it against the wall. It shattered, spraying bits of glass around the room. Aunty Doe leapt from the bed and headed for the open window, presumably to jump. Uncle Jim and the others sprang forward and grabbed her as I collapsed on the floor like a crumpled rag doll.

"Send me to a mental hospital," I sobbed.

Uncle Jim glared down at me, his arms folded stiffly across his chest, his face dark and unforgiving. "You're not going anywhere," he said.

My uncle and I sat in cold silence in the cab that brought us back to Riverside Drive. Up in the apartment, I walked through the foyer past the living room where my aunt's baby grand stood in the darkening gloom of evening. The piano was her pride and joy —and I was her greatest disappointment. I retreated down the hallway toward my room, expecting Uncle Jim to stop me at any moment. He didn't. His silence said it all. I was a disgrace in the eyes of my uncle, not only for my rebellious behavior, but more importantly, because I was guilty of breaking a serious rule. A white girl could not be with a black boy. Not in his world.

Hattie had always been a warm and loving presence in my life and I didn't share the feeling of superiority that my family displayed toward her kind. To me, that sort of thinking was part of the stifling provincialism I had left behind in Florida—where black people had to sit at the back of the bus, could not share public benches or bathrooms with whites, could not eat alongside whites at lunch counters at the five and dime. All the same, I was in disgrace. It seemed as if everything inside me had broken like the shattered vase in the hospital—and I wanted to pull back from life.

Mary Lee's mother, Lee, came to talk to me. We sat on the living room couch and she told me how I had my whole life ahead of me. How she had prayed about me to St. Jude, Patron Saint of Lost Causes.

I peeked at her sharp, no-nonsense face and watched her thin lips move. So I was a lost cause. Well, even so, she was throwing me a lifeline and I was grateful. A few days later, Aunty Doe came home from the hospital. The incident was never, ever mentioned again. I stayed in my room and it was weeks before I had any desire to venture out.

After that, I sometimes thought of Eddie Lewis and wondered exactly what had happened that day. The day I called him from the hospital. I found out that Mary Lee had been coerced into telling whom I had been with and where he could be found. I never tried to contact Eddie again. I'm sure my uncle and his friends must have scared him into forgetting about me, and who could blame him? Did they give him a beating? I just blocked it all out.

Uncle Jim dug up a psychiatrist. Some dusty old Freudian with a beard. After a few sessions, I got fed up with his embarrassing sexual questions and refused to go back. Something within me had fractured. Was I good or bad? Worthy or worthless? Princess or tramp?

With these feelings plaguing me, I made up my mind to immerse myself in the world that Bill Stephens had introduced me to—the curative world of music, theatre, art.

FIFTY-FIFTH STREET

Meanwhile, something was up in the underworld.

In 1956, Uncle Jim's good friend, Joe Adonis, was deported to Italy. His absence is believed to have weakened Frank Costello, who was billed during the Kefauver Hearings as Americas number one gangster. In May of the following year, a thug by the name of Vincent "The Chin" Gigante walked up to Costello, said, "This is for you, Frank," and fired a gun at his head, just grazing him. This convinced Costello that it was time to throw in the towel and he retired to a penthouse at the Waldorf Astoria.

That November Albert Anastasia, a Costello ally, was shot to death as he was getting a shave in the barbershop of the Park-Sheraton Hotel (formerly known as the Park Central—where, coincidentally, Arnold Rothstein had been murdered twenty-nine years earlier).

Three weeks after the Anastasia killing, on November 14th, a meeting of mobsters was held at the home of one Joseph "The

Barber" Barbara in Apalachin, New York. Local law enforcement raided the meeting—sending wise guys scurrying into the woods surrounding the estate. Many escaped into the night, but fifty-eight men were detained and indicted. They insisted they had come there after hearing that Mr. Barbara was *under the weather.* All were released. Although at least two of the men, Jerry Catena and Santo Trafficante, Jr., were friends of my uncle, forty years later Uncle Jim would say of the Apalachin meeting, "There was nobody there we knew." Obviously, this was a subject he didn't choose to go into.

According to Uncle Jim, he and Meyer couldn't have cared less about whatever gangland infighting may have been going on in New York. On December 10, 1957, Meyer's dream project, the Havana Riviera, opened for business. It is reported to have cost fourteen million to build and equip. Designed by Igor Boris Polevitzky, a dean of Miami Modern architecture, it was the most extravagant showplace in all of Havana. Two of Cuba's great artists, muralist Rolando Dirube, and sculptor Florencio Gelabert, lent their talents to the sophisticated décor. It was the first hotel in Cuba to have central air conditioning. The kitchen and dining room, always Meyer's special interest, were top of the line.

The casino had gold-leafed walls and a suspended ceiling from which hung seven over-sized crystal chandeliers. It was run by Dino Cellini, who had been our charming guide when I visited Cuba with my uncle in 1954. The Copa Cabaret Room opened with Ginger Rogers and her Musical Revue directed by Jack Cole. Meyer complained about Rogers, "She can wiggle her ass, but she can't sing a goddam note!"

A distinguished roster of stars performed in the Copa room: Abbott & Costello, Vic Damone, Steve Allen, Nat King Cole, to name a few. Among the patrons who stayed at the hotel were William Holden, Esther Williams, George Raft, and Ava Gardner (who was rumored to have dragged a bellhop into her bed).

The Riviera Hotel was Meyer's pride and joy—the culmination of his long-held desire to realize his most ambitious dreams. The hotel represented elegance and class—Havana in the grand manner. Meyer was in his element—but he couldn't have done it alone. There was a long list of investors: Las Vegas moguls, Moe Dalitz and Morris Kleinman, Wilbur Clark of the Las Vegas Desert Inn, Edward Levinson of the Fremont, Hyman Abrams and Morris Rosen of the Flamingo. Vincent "Jimmy Blue Eyes" was also an investor in the Riviera and, as always, was right by Meyer's side.

Several months after the opening of the Riviera Hotel, Meyer arrived in New York and was promptly arrested and taken to the West Fifty-Fourth Street police station where he was interrogated about the recent murder of Albert Anastasia. Getting nowhere with that line of questioning, the police charged him with vagrancy, even though he owned two homes and had over a grand in his pocket at the time of his arrest.

Although law enforcement officials speculated that Meyer Lansky had reason to want Anastasia eliminated because he was planning to move into gambling operations in Cuba, further investigation did not bear this out. There was never any real indication that Meyer had anything to do with the death of Anastasia. His murder, like that of Ben Siegel, has remained a mystery to this day.

THE RIVERSIDE DRIVE neighborhood had changed over the years and crime had become rampant. My uncle and aunt had moved there in the early Forties. It was there that they heard the news that America had been attacked at Pearl Harbor. Now it was a different world; and although she loved the place, my aunt decided it was time to move.

They considered buying an apartment—but in the end, realized that they couldn't expose themselves to the scrutiny of a co-op committee. So my aunt found another rental, this time in midtown Manhattan.

19 West Fifty-Fifth Street would be their New York home for the rest of their lives. It was not a particularly large apartment—not nearly as large as the one they were leaving. But it had a lovely, airy feeling.

The master bedroom had pale pink shantung silk on the walls and a bed with a carved gilt headboard worthy of Marie Antoinette. The smaller back bedroom was for me, and I decorated it in a contemporary style, pairing a cobalt blue Herman Miller chair and an old French writing desk left behind by the previous tenant—and got myself a Siamese cat that I named Lady Kasa, and I couldn't have been more pleased that she hated my aunt and viciously attacked her whenever she entered my room.

My aunt's main focus, other than her thwarted interest in turning me into a replica of herself, was her wardrobe. She was known for her excellent taste, and she used a personal shopper to assist with her clothing purchases. At this period of her life, my aunt began to remind me of the Duchess of Windsor. I sometimes wonder if she had subconsciously modeled herself after Wallace Simpson, the American divorcee who caused a king to abdicate his throne.

My aunt, being a woman of her generation, believed it was her job to make a good appearance in order to reflect her husband's success. She measured her worth in terms of Uncle Jim's importance. I, on the other hand, hated the concept that a woman had no inherent value as a person. My generation would reject the values of our parents—through the black revolution, the sexual revolution, women's lib.

All those things were waiting in the wings. But for now, I grappled with my aunt. The more she saw that the person I was becoming wasn't an extension of her, the more she tried to draw me into that mold, attempting to stifle me as she had repressed herself. I responded by experiencing attacks of anxiety.

One day I would come to understand that my aunt was a classic conservative with all the narrow-mindedness that I associate with that viewpoint. Uncle Jim, on the other hand, was a liberal thinker, a maverick. Maybe I didn't always agree with what he thought—but, at least *he thought*! And that, I respected.

UNCLE JIM HAD STEPPED in to help Mary Lee when her career was faltering. He brought her to his pal, George Wood, at William Morris—which led to her casting in *The Happiest Millionaire,* a Broadway play starring aging movie star Walter Pidgeon.

Uncle Jim enjoyed using his considerable connections to get people jobs. He also liked to help out in other ways, such as paying for funerals, giving advice, mediating disagreements, and giving money to people in need. This served two purposes. First, since fortune had smiled on him, he thought he should pass it on. Second, helping others massaged his ego.

With Mary Lee away on the road, I was left friendless. I was shy and stayed to myself, but I soon met someone who took me under his wing.

I met Carmine Terra who was understudying the role of Bernardo in the new musical, *West Side Story*. "I've found a great singing teacher and you've got to meet her," he told me.

Her name was Violeta and she spoke with utter self-confidence and conviction. For the next several years, I would listen with rapt attention to whatever she said.

Violeta had two daughters, Catherine and Antoinette—and a third, Marguerite, was soon to be born. Her husband was an operatic singer by the name of Albert Hall, an intense blow-hard of a man who scared the life out of me. Soon I was taking lessons and eating dinner with the family five days a week.

Violeta seemed to me to be all the things I would have wished for in a mother, had I had the choice. Surely, I had been born into the wrong family. This was where I *really* belonged—ensconced in a world of music and art. Not Uncle Jim's world of casinos, cigarettes, and scotch and soda. I belonged in the world of Rodgers & Hammerstein, Harold Arlen, and Kurt Weill.

Violeta made me throw my cigarettes away.

"Violeta only serves fresh vegetables. They're healthier than canned or frozen," I told my aunt.

"Bullshit!" she replied, sourly.

Aunty Doe wasn't happy about Violeta's presence in my life. According to my aunt, nothing was right about me. The way I dressed—"Like a beatnik!" The books I read—"They'll make you crazy." The way I sang—"Too high." The jazz, opera and classical music I loved—"What's wrong with Sinatra?"

It was becoming painfully clear to her that she was losing control of her show business fantasy—featuring me. When I was small and she was overseeing my dance lessons, having my costumes made, parading me out in my toe shoes, she was able to live in her shapeless dreams of stardom. But now, reality was intruding in the form of people and ideas that she didn't feel comfortable with. Luckily, Uncle Jim had no such qualms and was perfectly happy to promote my ambitions.

ONE DAY, as I moved across the floor in one of my dance classes, I was surprised to see George Wood standing at the far end of the studio in his impeccably tailored alpaca overcoat.

Later that evening, he called the apartment and announced to my uncle, "A new Gwen Verdon has been discovered!'

He meant me.

And so began my uncle's involvement in my "career development." I was about to be put through the meat-grinder of my uncle's need to "take care of" people. To Jimmy Blue Eyes, it was simple. "Get the kid a job." I was in danger of becoming "Mr. Big-Shot's niece."

George's first move was to put me in touch with a down-on-his-luck vocal coach. I met Al Segal at a West Side rehearsal studio. When I entered the room, I saw a gray-haired man seated at a battered upright piano. He proudly introduced himself as the person who had coached Ethel Merman. This immediately turned me off because I viewed Merman as a brassy screamer. I was no Ethel Merman, nor did I want to be. (This was before I was floored by her bravura performance in *Gypsy*.)

Al asked me to sing something, and I started with a quiet, pensive song:

"When I fall in love...it will be forever...or I'll ne-ver fall in love..."

"Nah, nah, nah," he bellowed. "You gotta give it some oomph!"

I stared at him, stunned.

"Ya gotta spice it up...use your arms...cross your heart...make it sincere," he yelled.

"But, that's not the way I want to sing," I blurted out. "I just can't do it that way."

"Who do you think you are? You don't look like Vivian Leigh! You don't sing like Edith Piaf! So who the hell do you think you are?"

The next thing I knew, he was crying and telling me how his wife had run off with a musician. He was broke. His life was a shambles and he was having a breakdown.

I got out of there as quickly as I could.

Later that evening, Uncle Jim asked me how it went with Al Segal —"Known him for years, a great guy!"

When I tried to explain that the whole thing had turned into an embarrassing disaster, he just shrugged his shoulders. "What's the big deal?" he asked.

To Uncle Jim, nothing was a problem. He had all the sensitivity of an ice cube.

Next, George told my uncle that I should study acting. In those days, the actor John Cassavettes had a school on Forty-Fifth Street in the theatre district. It was the usual type of broken-down place, up a rickety flight of stairs to dusty studios. The person in charge was a man by the name of Burt Lane. (This was long before his daughter, Diane, was born. She would become a child actress and, later, a movie star.) He interviewed me and assigned me to a beginner class taught by a blond-haired fellow named Sandy. I showed up for my first class in total fear.

The initial assignment for a new student was to memorize and perform a monologue. I chose one from the play, *The Rainmaker*. Week after week, I attended class, watched the work of the other students, and listened to Sandy talk about sense memory and other such acting tools. Each week, he asked me if I was ready and, each week, my answer was, "No."

I finally worked up the courage to take the stage.

In the grip of fear, I delivered a monologue from *The Rainmaker* as if in a trance. The next thing I remember is Sandy staring up at me.

"That was really heavy," he said.

I didn't exactly know what "heavy" meant, but it seemed like whatever happened while I was in that trancelike state turned out pretty good.

Not long after that, one cold, gray day, Burt Lane asked me to come next door to the coffee shop because he wanted to speak to me.

We sat down in one of the grubby booths and I ordered a cup of tea. I was very uneasy because I was sixteen and he was a mature man.

"Carole," he started, staring intently at me, "It's been brought to my attention that you have a certain quality...I think there's a possibility we can do something with you."

I sipped my tea nervously.

"I want you to listen to what I say. I would like you to put yourself completely in my hands."

I didn't know what he was talking about, but he scared the hell out of me. Had George Wood put him up to something? Was he trying to put the make on me? Or did he actually mean what he had said?

Whichever it was—I got out of there as soon as I could, and never returned to the Cassavetes School.

UNCLE JIM, MATCHMAKER

We were staying at the Sands Hotel, of which Uncle Jim owned a piece. There were certain things I just knew. I knew that my uncle's old friend and partner, Ben Siegel, had been paramount in the creation of Las Vegas as the gaming capital of America, just as my uncle and his pals had played an important role in the popularization of South Florida. If not them, who else was going to supply a glitzy place for the public to gamble, dine, and be entertained? The whole party atmosphere of the clubs and casinos was a natural progression of Prohibition. The difference between Las Vegas and Florida was that in Nevada, gambling was *legal*.

THE FIRST EVENING we were there, we were met ceremoniously by Jack Entratter. The sign at the front of the building read *Jack Entratter's Sands*—but I knew that he was only the "front man." Behind the scenes, individuals who had records or reputations that prevented them from being publicly acknowledged as partners held points.

Entratter had once been a bouncer at the Copacabana in New York. He was a big bear of a man, and he led us into the main showroom where we ordered dinner and watched Jayne Mansfield's husband, Mickey Hargitay, carry her around on his beefy shoulders on the mainstage.

Everything about Las Vegas seemed cheesy to me. After dinner, we went into the casino where my aunt put her "gambling" glove on her right hand and settled in to play the slot machine. I sat pouting in a plush chair, making no effort to mask my disgust. While energy popped all around me in the form of card players, crap shooters, cocktail waitresses, and frenetic music wafting in from the nearby lounge—I was wearing my bored face. I could never understand gambling as a pastime, since losing is inevitable because the odds are always on the side of the "house."

One night, while my aunt and I were sitting in the Sands lounge, Sammy Davis, Jr. approached us. He had come to Uncle Jim several years before because he was in trouble with club owners in Chicago. Davis had overbooked himself and was trying to tell these people that he couldn't fulfill the engagement at that time. They threatened to break his legs.

Playing his role as the great mediator, Uncle Jim stepped in and told the Chicago tough guys to lay off Sammy.

"They were just tryin' to scare him," was the way Uncle Jim explained it.

Sammy came over to pay his respects to my aunt. He couldn't have been nicer as he kneeled down beside my chair to speak to me, as well. His warmth was infectious off stage as well as on. Uncle Jim thought well of him, saying, "The kid has the 'gift of gab'—he's okay."

The Sands was the first place to allow Sammy to *stay* where he was performing, rather than being housed in a black neighborhood. He had suffered that indignity all his life.

At the time, he was in love with the movie star, Kim Novak. Their romance was cut short when Harry Cohn, head of Columbia Pictures, got wind of it and turned to mob-connected Johnny Roselli to deliver an ultimatum to Davis. "Marry a black woman immediately or pay the consequences."

"Please give Jimmy my very best regards," Sammy told my aunt with great sincerity that night. Then off he went, his skin-tight tuxedo reflecting the glow from the chandeliers that illuminated the room.

BACK IN NEW YORK, Uncle Jim decided to become a matchmaker. While Aunty Doe and I were in Vegas, we met Teddy Randazzo, who was performing at one of the hotels. Uncle Jim knew him and thought he was a "nice Italian kid." The nice kid was an up and coming rock & roll singer/composer who would go on to have a long, successful career and write many hit songs, including the classic rock hit, "Goin Out of My Head."

Uncle Jim invited Teddy, who lived in New York, over to the apartment. He dutifully showed up and spent an uncomfortable couple of hours with the three of us. Mostly, he sat at the piano, trying to *play* as much as *possible*. Regardless of what Uncle Jim may have had in mind, neither Teddy nor I had any interest in each other; but Teddy was a good sport about it and a very nice guy.

∽

GEORGE WOOD PUT me in the hands of an agent by the name of Bernie Styles. Bernie handled film extras. My first job was on a popular television drama called *Suspicion.* These were the days of the Golden Age of television. Shows were aired *live* and it was electrifying for me to watch a perspiring Burgess Meredith fly from one set to the next, changing costumes on the run.

Next, Bernie Styles called with a film job. *That Kind of Woman* starred Sophia Loren, Tab Hunter, and George Sanders—and was directed by Sidney Lumet. We worked at numerous locations all around the city, and I was able to observe Sophia Loren who seemed genuinely earthy and had a very hearty laugh that could be heard a mile away.

∽

GEORGE WOOD CALLED and said he was sending me on an audition. It was for a movie called *Country Music Festival,* and they were casting dancers.

How I overcame my fear and survived that audition I'll never know—but, somehow, I managed to get through it and was cast in this low-budget movie, starring the oddest assortment of talent— headed by Zsa Zsa Gabor, Rocky Graziano, and Patty Duke. It was my first job as a professional dancer— a dream fulfilled.

∽

ONE DAY, out of the blue, my aunt said, "Let's go up and visit Bill Stephens."

I was surprised at that and couldn't figure out what motivated her. But on a bright, autumn day, we boarded a train for the two-hour ride to the Yale Psychiatric Institute in New Haven, Connecticut. I hadn't seen Bill since the craziness in Florida, when Bill's father had hustled him off—practically in a straightjacket.

I stared out the window and wondered what it would be like to see him again. At the hospital, we were shown to his floor and were shocked to discover that none of the rooms had doors.

"What about privacy?" I asked Bill, after the first awkward moments had passed.

"Well, a couple of weeks ago one of the *inmates* (Bill gleefully emphasized the word) managed to slit his throat with a sharp object. I guess safety trumps privacy."

Aunty Doe and I were silent.

"Oh, yeah," Bill continued. "When I want to use my palette knife for painting, I have to have a nurse babysit me." He grinned at this, but the grin didn't seem attached to his face. It was sad to see him in this place, especially since I didn't completely understand why he was there.

NOT LONG AFTER OUR VISIT, the hospital started letting Bill out for weekend trips to New York. He had been diagnosed with schizophrenia, but he seemed fine to me. He'd arrive on a Saturday morning and sit at the dining table with my aunt, drinking coffee and talking for hours, while he waited for me to get up. Sometimes, if she had somewhere to go, he would come into my bedroom and make me laugh with stories about *the nuthouse*, as he called it.

"Hey, Pieface—you should have seen what happened in group last week. There's this girl who never speaks. All she does is rock back and forth in her chair all day long. Well, last week, right in the middle of group—she had an orgasm!"

We laughed and laughed about that.

Bill stayed with his friend, Jo Freeman, whom he knew from The Art Student's League. Jo had a commercial art studio on West Forty-Fifth Street, above an Italian Restaurant called La Strada. He lived over the restaurant, and that's where Bill would stay when he was in town. We had many afternoon delights in that apartment; then, we would run downstairs to La Strada to enjoy baked ziti, wine, and tiramisu. One evening, we spotted Arthur Miller sitting with friends, a few tables away from us. Being so close to this giant of the theatre, I could hardly eat.

These were the days before the massive influx of immigrants into New York and before homelessness overflowed the Bowery and came uptown. On weekends, a wonderful stillness would settle over the city. Bill and I strolled around, visiting museums, especially the Museum of Modern Art around the corner. Wandering with no particular destination, we paused to browse in old bookstores and regularly passed Moondog, a blind giant, wrapped in rags, who stood guard enigmatically on the corner of Fifty-Fifth and Sixth.

THE MORE I developed interests that didn't coincide with hers, the more bitter my aunt became. She was resentful of Bill and my voice teacher, Violeta, both of whom were influencing me. However, at this time the only complaint she voiced about Bill was that his pants were too tight, which seemed to annoy her.

As Uncle Jim went about his usual business (whatever that was)—Aunty Doe hung out with Bill in the mornings while I slept. She would linger over her tepid cup of coffee in her robe or housedress, a hairnet wrapped around her head to preserve her do, a patch, meant to prevent wrinkles, stuck between her eyes. I can only imagine that she must have been taking some pleasure in his company, tight pants or not.

I HAD a plan for my eighteenth birthday. So on the last morning of July, I announced to my aunt and uncle, "I'm getting married today."

After a deadly pause, my aunt yelled, "Stop her, Jimmy!"

"The hell with her. Let her do whatever she wants."

My aunt ran her hands through her unkempt morning hair and rushed to the kitchen, where she grabbed the ironing board from the pantry and set it up. Uncle Jim had just come back from getting fresh rolls from the French bakery across the street and the daily paper from the newsstand next door. In his well-cut trousers and fine cotton sport shirt, he remained the picture of cool, unflappable composure, as my aunt went mad.

There, in the kitchen with its timeworn black and white linoleum and the cabinets that never quite closed, she ironed. In front of the old enamel sink, the unused copper measuring cups hung on hooks, the empty breadbox, she ironed furiously. She never cooked in that kitchen— didn't really know how. But she ironed the kitschy kitchen towels with the pink and yellow poodles, the linen handkerchiefs embroidered with her initial: *F* for Florence. She ironed as if by doing so she could straighten out all the mistakes and missteps of the past. "Stop her, Jimmy," she wailed.

My uncle, the mediator, spoke in an unruffled voice. "Take it easy, Flo. There's nothing you can do about it. Carole's gonna have to learn the hard way."

I wanted to get the hell out of that apartment. To walk away from my uncle, my aunt, the grand piano, the silk drapes, the silver, the outer order masking inner chaos. My heart was pounding as I walked into the living room where Uncle Jim sat in his comfortable chair with *The Daily News* perched on his lap.

"Bill and I are getting married in the church across from Violeta's apartment house. She and her husband are standing up for me. You're welcome to be there if you want."

"I guess you don't give a damn about what you're doing to your aunt," he said, icily.

Uncle Jim, in his quiet way, managed to control those around him. Not by fear, but by some inner strength of personality. It was uncomfortable to oppose him, but I was firm in my resolve.

"Nobody is going to stop me from living my life," I said, staring him down.

He looked back at me with hard eyes. "Tell me one right thing you've ever done in your life," he said. I had never before been on the receiving end of that stone-cold gaze.

Tears stung my eyes as I walked out of the apartment into the dim hallway and stood waiting for the elevator that was coming to take me into my future. I would remember his remark. It cut like hell because it went to the heart of my deep belief in my own worthlessness.

Uncle Jim did come to my simple wedding, after all. Sadly, my aunt did not. I think on that day, all her dreams of the brilliant destiny she had envisioned for me, died. She had never understood—but I could not live *her life* or *her dream*. I needed to discover my own dreams within myself—a self I had yet to find.

AVA SAT HERE!

The scent of change was in the air. The buttoned-down Fifties would soon give way to the turbulent, revolutionary Sixties. As the new decade roared from one year to the next, fueled by marches, riots, and assassinations, my uncle and aunt seemed to become more and more out of sync with the times.

They were well into middle age in an era when sixty was not yet the new fifty, and they were living a settled, almost ordinary life. Aunty Doe went from brunette to blonde. Uncle Jim was—Uncle Jim. After my marriage, they began spending three or four months of the year in Florida again. Aunty Doe redecorated the house, obliterating the glorious old Forties décor and replacing it with glitz and gilt.

When they visited Las Vegas, they followed their old custom of traveling separately, evidently in the belief that the world would never be able to recover from the loss of both of them. Aunty Doe still stayed at the Sands, where she could indulge her habit of playing the slot machines, complete with her white blister-busting glove. Uncle Jim laid low at Cousin Larry's house, since he was on the Vegas "verboten" list and couldn't be seen in the hotels or casinos. He was perfectly happy to spend his time reading, playing billiards with Larry's three teen-aged sons, allowing his tender-hearted daughter-in-law, Frannie, to dote on him.

THE CONVENTION of marriage meant nothing to me—but I thought marrying Bill would provide the key to the life in art for which I yearned. My mother had allowed her sister and brother-in-law to impinge on our relationship. My father was incapable of any kind of normal family life. I felt smothered by my aunt, who resented every thought, impulse, or behavior of mine that deviated from hers. And finally, though I could not help but admire Uncle Jim as a strong individual who lived by his own rules—his motto seemed to be, "Do as I say, not as I do." He didn't have the capacity to empathize with anything outside his range of experience and could quickly lose interest in anyone who didn't need his "help." He had the ability to detach and he could dismiss you with a shrug of his shoulders.

I wanted to separate myself from Uncle Jim and the rest of my family. However, I would find the establishment of an independent identity more easily said than done.

HAVING NO OTHER PROSPECTS, Bill agreed to go to work for his father, who had developed a traveling sales program for *Esquire Magazine*. After a few months, Bill and I took an apartment in the suburb of Evanston, Illinois, where I auditioned for the First

National Company of *West Side Story*. After three grueling days of auditions, I did not get the show.

If I had known better, I would have viewed this as nothing more than a temporary setback, the kind of disappointment that goes with the territory in show business. But since I had been led to believe that *I should get what I wanted when I wanted it*, this blow took on the finality of death. My failure to be cast in *West Side Story* brought up deep feelings of inadequacy and the suspicion that everyone who had ever said I had talent *had lied*. The show moved on to the next location, and Bill and I decided that we'd had enough of Chicago. I was depressed and didn't much care where I was.

My uncle and aunt were elated when we returned to New York. As far as they were concerned, I had descended from potential star to house-frau the moment I chose to get married. I knew my aunt was secretly heartbroken. And, in my head, I could just hear my uncle say, with a shrug, "I tried to help her," dismissing the whole matter in his narcissistic way—as if he thought that everything depended solely on *his* involvement.

UNCLE JIM WASTED no time in arranging a job for Bill. He spoke to his friends, Ralph Watkins and Moe Lewis, who owned a popular nightspot, Basin Street East, where Bill was put to work creating murals of New Orleans-style jazz musicians on the interior walls of the club. After that, he remained on the payroll, making himself useful in a variety of ways, which included spending time rubbing the neck of the great Peggy Lee, who, according to Bill, downed the best part of a bottle of Brandy every night before she wrapped herself in a feather boa and went onstage.

Bill and I moved into an old theatrical hotel on Fifty-Sixth Street, behind Carnegie Hall, where Faith Dane, our outrageous next-door neighbor befriended me. Faith had originated the role of Mazeppa, the stripper with the trumpet in *Gypsy*. Now, here I was, hanging out in her room almost every afternoon with my legs thrown over the arm of a lumpy couch while I listened to her frenetic chatter:

"Oh, yeah, doll, you should have been there when I auditioned for Jerome Robbins. See, I was doin' an act, at the time, and I had this special material that I had written for me. So I go in and do this bit for them and they go crazy. They wound up hiring me—and, using my stuff!"

"So you're saying 'bump it with a trumpet,' and all that, was your material?"

"That's right!" Faith bellowed.

One afternoon, Faith made me an offer. "Listen, kid. Pretty soon I'm gonna' be goin' on the road and I'll be headed out to Vegas. I'm gonna take a couple a' girls with me. It'll be a little nudie, but what would you think about joining the act?"

It was sweet of her to ask. But I was newly married and pregnant—so I would hardly have run off to Vegas at that point. Not to mention that the "nudie" thing was out of the question.

Faith was truly an original. Years later, I learned from reading remarks made by Arthur Laurents, one of the creators of *Gypsy*, she had originally ended her act by sticking the horn up her ass and blowing!

WITH A BABY ON THE WAY, Bill and I started hunting for an apartment. We envisioned an arty loft where Bill could paint and we could begin our *real* life. We found a little walk-up on the Upper West Side, which, in those pre-Lincoln Center days, had yet to be gentrified and was a rough area of tenement row houses. Full of enthusiasm, we rushed over to Fifty-Fifth Street to ask Uncle Jim for his help.

My aunt jumped up from her chair and grabbed a cigarette. "Jimmy, that's a lousy neighborhood," she gasped. "I don't want Carole living in some crappy place where her life will be threatened every time she goes out!"

"For Christ's sake, Flo, will you calm down?" Uncle Jim switched the ever-present toothpick from one side of his mouth to the other and thought for a minute. "George Wood's apartment is available. Why don't you move in there? Doesn't that make more sense now that a baby's coming?"

"I don't want to move into George Wood's apartment!" I protested.

"Well, that's what I think you should do," he said, in a maddeningly reasonable tone.

Since we didn't have the money to make the move on our own, we allowed ourselves to be persuaded—and moved into swanky 40 Central Park South. There, we settled in, two failed bohemians, to await the birth of our child.

I didn't know it then, but I had just made a grave misstep in the journey of my life. This was where I needed to strike out on my own. Sever the umbilical cord. Become my own person. And my husband was supposed to support me in that process. Instead, Bill got on the raft with me and we sailed blithely along together in the wrong direction.

Having failed to break away from my family's influence, Bill and I found ourselves living in George's small, one-bedroom apartment filled with cast-off furniture that had belonged to George's sister, Sparky.

The only thing that saved it from being a total loss was that it had previously been used by Frank Sinatra as a pied-a-terre when he was in town and Ava Gardner had frequently stayed there. Every time I sat on the john, I thought, "Ava sat here!" We got rid of Sinatra's Japanese shoji screens, left the mirrored bedroom wall, and settled in to await the birth of our baby.

Jack E. Leonard, Sonny King with Jimmy

As my pregnancy progressed, I continued to take dance class and Mary Lee often accompanied me. Afterwards, we would walk over and join my uncle and aunt and their friends for a bite to eat at Lindy's. Since the early Twenties, Lindy's, the best and most famous of New York's delis, had been a favorite hangout of show folk and the underworld. Damon Runyon was a big fan and wrote the restaurant into his stories thinly disguised as "Mindy's."

The table was always filled with fragrant dishes of pickles, sweet coleslaw, and baskets of onion, pumpernickel, and raisin bread—accompanied by big slabs of butter swimming in icy water. Mary Lee and I would order fat roast beef sandwiches slathered with Russian dressing or steaming bowls of matzo ball soup.

The evenings at Lindy's were punctuated by the appearance of celebrities at our table. One evening, it was Mike Todd with his wife, Elizabeth Taylor, who came over to pay their respects. (He was loud, she was quiet.) Uncle Jim had turned down his request for investment capital for *Around the World in 80 Days*, but Todd didn't hold a grudge. Lovable Jimmy Durante was often around and comedian Jack E. Leonard, with his staccato delivery of insulting one-liners, was a regular who could leave the whole table weeping with laughter. He spared no one, not even Uncle Jim, who laughed the loudest of all.

One night, Marty Jurow showed up to spill some secrets of the stars. Jurow had been an agent at William Morris, and produced a string of successful movies such as *The Fugitive Kind, The Pink Panther*, and *Breakfast at Tiffany's*. He captured the table's attention as he described the actor, Jack Palance, picking up his kids in Central Park. Because of his malevolent appearance, he was mistaken for a kidnapper. He talked about how Sophia Loren had done anything she could to survive during and after the war and how Anthony Quinn discovered her working as an extra at Cinecitta Studios in Rome, took her "under his wing" and launched her career. He went on at length about Frank Sinatra.

According to Jurow, Sinatra caught his wife, Ava Gardner, in bed with Lana Turner— and tried to shoot himself because of it.

I was accustomed to seeing the famous as well as the not-so-famous lining up to rub elbows with my uncle. He was the celebrity's celebrity. But I had an uncomfortable aversion to being part of Uncle Jim's retinue. In the midst of the parade of people who seemed to want to be in Uncle Jim's presence, my ego was such that I did not wish to be an appendage of him or my aunt.

WHEN I CALLED my aunt to say that my water broke, she was so nervous that she tripped on the curb as she headed for a cab on the way to the hospital, cutting a gash in her leg. Uncle Jim, walking behind her, made a typical heartfelt comment, "I told ya' to watch your step, Flo."

My uncle and aunt insisted that the baby be christened. They were the ultimate godparents and had performed that service many times in the past for the children of friends. They were my godparents as well and they considered it a serious responsibility.

My aunt clung to the shards of her Catholicism even though, as a divorcee, she could not receive Communion and was not considered married to Uncle Jim in the eyes of the church. He, although a confirmed atheist, saw no harm in the christening of babies. So on a bright spring morning, we all traveled downtown to the Church of Saint Raphael where baby Shawn was christened by Father Bob Pirella, AKA the show business priest. Father Bob sported a nose job and traveled frequently to Vegas where he hobnobbed with celebrities and wise guys. He hung out in Lindy's and the barbershop in the Warwick Hotel. After he published his memoirs, his superiors transferred him far, far away from Manhattan.

Bill and I saw no harm in going along with the christening ceremony, which we viewed as a quaint tradition.

At that point, I wasn't seeing the contradictory nature of my life. Living in Frank Sinatra's vacated apartment, having my baby christened by the Damon Runyon priest. What had happened to my vision of the *bohemian artist's life?* My family's influence was like an undertow that kept pulling me back.

ORDER OF THE CLOOM

George Wood had been close to Frank Sinatra ever since the singer—suffering over the demise of his marriage to Ava Gardner—tried to end it all by cutting his wrists in the New York apartment of songwriter Jimmy Van Heusen. Sinatra's career had just begun to rise from the ashes after the release of From *Here to Eternity*, in which he portrayed the role of Maggio, a skinny, scrappy Italian much like himself. Before that, his relationship with Columbia Records had soured; but he signed a deal with Capital Records and his career was moving forward again. The William Morris Agency had recently picked him up at the time when the attempted suicide took place and George Wood was given the job of looking after him as he carried the torch for Ava.

"So, George, do you also wipe his ass when he goes to the bathroom?" Uncle Jim liked to joke.

The subject of Frank Sinatra came up frequently in my uncle's circle. Uncle Jim's friend, Henrí Giné, worked for Sinatra as part of his team of East Coast representatives. Since Henrí and his wife,

Billie, were close to Sinatra's parents, Dolly and Marty, my uncle and aunt became friendly with them as well. They were quite fond of the elder Sinatras, especially Dolly, a larger-than-life character who could swear like a longshoreman. I remember meeting Sinatra and observing a small, immaculate man with ruddy, scrubbed skin, startlingly blue eyes and a noticeable scar behind his ear.

Jimmy with Dolly & Marty Sinatra

There's been a lot of speculation about Sinatra's relationship with "the boys." I've even read somewhere that Uncle Jim was his "best mob friend." Actually, they were nothing more than acquaintances. They *knew of* each other more than they *knew* each other. Their two universes had intersected, and they certainly had mutual friends. But as time went on, Uncle Jim began to hear that Sinatra could act like a bully. That he pushed people around (like waiters, for instance) who couldn't defend themselves. That he went around with an entourage of so-called tough guys meant to intimidate. Uncle Jim heard these things through the grapevine and he thought it was shitty behavior.

There's a widely held belief that Frank Sinatra was part of the underworld. As an entertainer, he certainly knew a lot of the wise guys who were in a position to employ him. And if people wanted to paint him with the same brush—well, evidently, that suited his over-sized ego just fine.

It's been said that Harry Cohn, the head of Metro-Goldwyn-Mayer Studios, was forced to use Sinatra in *From Here to Eternity* because of mob pressure. Marty Jurow credits *himself* with being the conduit between Cohn and Jimmy Blue Eyes. He even quotes Uncle Jim as saying, "He owes us."

It makes a good story, but questioning my uncle some forty years later, he told me in no uncertain terms, "Ava Gardner got the role for Sinatra. Sinatra couldn't even get himself arrested, and she was a big star at the time. Harry Cohn wanted to keep her happy."

GEORGE WOOD BEGAN DATING a blonde Grace Kelly look-alike named Lois O'Brien. Although he was sixty-plus and she was in her mid-twenties, it was just par for the course. George was famous for showing up every couple of weeks with a different young starlet on his arm. When he let it be known that marriage was being considered, his friends were in a state of disbelief. Sure enough, in January of 1958, despite the fact that George was Jewish and divorced, he and Lois took their vows at St. Malachy's Roman Catholic Church, known as the "actor's chapel." Father Bob did the honors, with Jimmy Blue Eyes serving as best man. The characters would have been right at home in a tale by Damon Runyon.

Lois transformed George's life and he seemed madly smitten with her. The rooms in their large, airy apartment were filled with fresh flowers, and Lois always wore a flower tucked into the fold of her French twist. In restaurants, George would burst into song and everyone at the table would have to suffer through his terrible rendition of, *"Look at that face, just look at it. Look at that fabulous face of yours"*—while Lois broke into a Colgate grin.

Since Bill and I had no social life (and also because we liked to eat well) we wound up spending a lot of time with my uncle and aunt and their cronies at Dinty Moore's or Frankie & Johnny's. We would often finish up the evening in George and Lois's apartment, along with Lois's mother who was a frequent houseguest.

Being around George wasn't hard to take. He was a funny, devil-may-care kind of guy. He invented an imaginary club called the Cloom, and he once presented my uncle and aunt with a large, loving cup engraved:

-TO JIMMY AND FLO-
CONGRATULATIONS ON TWENTY-FIVE YEARS OF BLISS
FROM THE ORDER OF THE CLOOM

Sometimes, unexpectedly, George would say, "Jimmy, I think we should call a meeting of the Order of the Cloom. I'll bring three or four broads and we'll discuss the important issues of the day."

"Don't flatter yourselves," my aunt would mutter, between sips of Campari.

Lois was a singer with an ambitious stage mother who often came to stay with the newlyweds. George wasn't crazy about that and he liked to amuse his friends with complaints that his mother-in-law (a woman of his age) was pilfering things like ashtrays and custom-made shirts and sneaking them out of the apartment in her suitcase. He would jokingly complain that Lois's mother cramped their sex life. According to him, when she was around, he had to get rid of those four Chinamen that he usually employed to lift him on and off his bride.

Although Lois was only slightly older than I was, she was definitely a lot wiser. Somehow, in spite of our vast differences, we fell into an unlikely friendship.

We both had babies and Lois and I would sometimes cross Fifty-Ninth Street together and push our baby carriages down to the lake in the park. Despite the fact that my aunt had worried and wondered how I would ever adjust to motherhood, I found that being a mother gave me a sense of purpose that I had never previously experienced.

ONE DAY, as we sat together on a park bench, Lois enlightened me as to how she became acquainted with my uncle. "When I first began dating George," she said, "he introduced Jimmy as a lawyer. I used to throw small dinner parties and Jimmy would attend them with his lady friend."

His lady friend? My stomach fell into my shoes, but I put on a poker face and kept listening.

"Once we decided to get married," she continued, "George was forced to come clean and tell me who Jimmy really was—and that he had a wife. It was only then that he introduced me to Flo."

I couldn't believe this, but I said nothing. Just kept watching the ducks swimming in the lake.

Lois went on to describe a recent evening when the usual gang was gathered in the lobby of the Hotel St. Moritz before going next door to the Café de la Paix for dinner. She said that my uncle and aunt were there, along with her and George, Doc Rosen and Henrí and Billie Giné. Everyone in the group, with the exception of my aunt, knew that the blonde woman who passed by and waved "hello" was Uncle Jim's *special friend*.

I felt physically sick. I was aware that in the distant past he had strayed, but I was shocked and disgusted to find out that it was still going on. And with the knowledge of all their friends!

At that moment, I understood instinctively that my aunt *knew*. Suddenly, it became clear how stoicism must have hardened her and turned her into the brittle person I found so difficult to like.

COSA NOSTRA

By the late Fifties, the good fortune that had, up to that time, been enjoyed by Uncle Jim and Meyer was beginning to go awry. On the evening of December 31, 1958, Fidel Castro, leading his band of revolutionaries, took control of Cuba and Fulgencio Batista fled to the Dominican Republic. When news of the takeover reached the people, they stormed into the streets to celebrate. In some areas, violence broke out.

Contrary to the episode presented in Francis Ford Coppola's *Godfather II*, Meyer Lansky did not receive advance notice of the oncoming menace. It was in the early morning hours that he and his wife, Teddy, heard the bad news. As workers in the hotel deserted their jobs to join the neighborhood celebrations, Meyer went to work in the kitchen, giving out food to the bewildered guests. Teddy rolled up her sleeves and began mopping the marble floors in a futile effort to clean up the muddy footprints of *pigs*, brought into the hotel by peasants whose actions conveyed both curiosity and contempt.

Three days later, Meyer and Teddy flew to Miami; but by the end of January he was back in Havana, hoping to forge a relationship with the new regime.

Although Castro, at first, announced his intention of removing the Yankee gangster/casino owners from Havana, he was soon persuaded to change his mind when several thousand dealers, croupiers, and restaurant and bar workers paraded through the streets protesting the loss of their jobs.

When Castro arrived in New York in April, he was seen as the liberator who had ousted the corrupt Batista regime and he received a hero's welcome. Meyer was cautiously optimistic, until his brother, Jake, and Jake's right-hand-man, Dino Cellini, were arrested and imprisoned in Havana. They were released a few days later, but Meyer was reading the writing on the wall.

He commented to his lawyer, Joe Varon, "Somebody should warn the government what's going on in Cuba."

Varon told him, "Well, Meyer, I think that somebody is you."

Varon arranged a meeting at his Hollywood office with Meyer and several local agents of the FBI. Meyer explained that, based on what he had observed, he believed American journalists and politicians were unaware of the true nature of the "liberators." He warned that, "Before long, the entire government of Cuba will be communistic."

One can only imagine what these FBI agents thought of Meyer's efforts to enlighten them. They were probably puzzled as to what his motives might be and his warnings certainly went unheeded. True, Meyer stood to lose a great deal in Cuba. But what could be done about that? Why should he stick his neck out and go to the FBI? The answer is that Meyer cared about what happened to America and he was concerned about national security.

Castro opened diplomatic relations with Moscow a year later, and Meyer's predictions about Cuba proved to be all too accurate. He had staked everything on the success of the Riviera Hotel. It was his crowning achievement and now it was over almost before it had begun. Although he rarely spoke about his losses, they were monumental.

He put it in very simple terms. "I crapped out."

THE EARLY SIXTIES would be years of transition for Jimmy and Flo. Hattie passed away too young. Little Niggie Flax, who had been an endearing presence at Monroe Street during my adolescence, sharing every meal with us, went to meet "that big bookie in the sky." Flo and Grace's step-father, Harry Gelinas, died in Florida and was laid to rest at Calvary Cemetery on Long Island, alongside my grandmother. The burial was attended by FBI surveillance.

1962 turned out to be a significant year for Uncle Jim because of Joseph Valachi. A convicted heroin trafficker and semi-illiterate thug, Valachi beat a fellow inmate to death with an iron pipe. Already having a reputation as a guy who said too much, Valachi had no trouble cutting a deal to testify about all he allegedly knew concerning the mob. He explained the inner workings of the upper echelon of organized crime to the Senate Permanent Subcommittee on Investigations—even though, as an underworld small fry, he was hardly in a position to do so. Interestingly, he pooh-poohed the word "mafia," saying that no one in organized crime referred to it by that name.

"We say 'Cosa Nostra,'" he explained to John McClellan, the committee chairman. *Cosa Nostra*, meaning roughly in Italian "this thing of ours," would become the new catchphrase, a title that journalists, authors, and filmmakers could hang their hats on.

"We say 'Cosa Nostra!'"

Who did he mean by "we?" Was he just commenting on an oft-used street expression? Did he invent it? No matter, 'Cosa Nostra' entered into the lexicon of American speech.

Known as a teller of tall tales, Valachi saved himself from the death penalty—and brought himself to national prominence—by coming up with lurid stories of the underworld that would fuel the mythology beyond anything that my uncle or his cohorts could have imagined.

The Valachi Papers, a "memoir" written a few years later by crime writer, Peter Maas, caused the FBI to heighten their focus on the mob; and in a matter of a few years, more members of the syndicate (assuming there *was* a syndicate) had been jailed than in the last thirty years.

In the book, Valachi described Jimmy Blue Eyes with white knuckles, holding a rope around a man's neck in the back of a delivery truck. Uncle Jim's comment was, "He told 'em what they wanted to hear. I'm only a two-dollar bum—and that bastard is dirt under my feet."

It was during this period that the study of organized crime really began to heat up—based on hearsay, conjecture, and a large dose of imagination. The various law enforcement agencies involved came up with a somewhat military structure, complete with ranks and procedures. Unable to conceive of a loosely connected web of partners, friends, and entrepreneurs who looked for opportunities to make money—they envisioned a powerful, fully organized cartel of monumental proportions.

ME AND JIMMY BLUE EYES

These were the years when my uncle was hounded by the FBI. They tapped his phones. They sat in their cars for hours watching the Monroe Street house. On one occasion, an agent even came to the door, rang the doorbell, and asked for a cup of coffee. "Get lost," was the reply.

Sometimes, for laughs, Uncle Jim would drive around Hollywood or Hallandale for an hour or so, just to lead the agents on a merry chase.

Coming face to face with an agent while picking up the evening paper at Breeding's Drugstore, Uncle Jim threw him a remark. "Is this what you went to college for—to follow a bum like me around all day long?"

What to think of all the rumors? Stories, books, news reports, naming Jimmy Blue Eyes as a top-level member of the Genovese crime family. All I know is that I never once heard the name Vito Genovese mentioned by my uncle, and I have no reason to believe that he belonged to any network or organization in New York or elsewhere.

I know for sure what his opinion was of John Gotti and his generation of wise guys. He thought they were morons. Just the fact that they seemed to seek instead of avoid publicity was, to my uncle, proof of their idiocy. Based on what I've been able to observe over a lifetime, Jimmy and Meyer came to Florida after the demise of Prohibition, seeking to escape from the past, to make money, and in the process, to make a new life for themselves.

I would like to think that they dealt with the mayhem of the Prohibition days because they *had* to. In other words, they were in it but not of it. As soon as they could, they started that new life under the circumstance available to them. They knew and understood gambling and that became their business. As for Uncle Jim, whatever created his tough reputation, it stayed with him, to a great extent, for the rest of his life.

∼

WHEN JOHN KENNEDY WAS ASSASSINATED, the whole country mourned; but Uncle Jim couldn't have cared less.

In those days, the public was in the dark about much of what went on, but Uncle Jim knew a lot about the Kennedys. Public figures were, for the most part, able to suppress knowledge of their private lives. Uncle Jim was ahead of his time with information that would later become widely known. He was familiar with old Joe Kennedy's beginnings as a bootlegger. Uncle Jim believed that the voracious ambition that he projected onto his sons eventually brought tragedy upon the family. Kennedy wanted one of his sons to be President, and he did everything in his power to make that happen. The cost proved to be very high and was an indictment against the old man, in my uncle's eyes.

He was also aware of the philandering of the Kennedy men. It wasn't a moral judgment. My uncle took for granted that it was the nature of men to behave that way. It was more that he thought they were phonies and hypocrites, holding themselves up to be better than the next man. High enough, even, to lead the nation.

Uncle Jim was friendly with Joe DiMaggio, who confided in him about his hatred of the Kennedys. He told my uncle about the despicable goings-on at the Cal-Neva Lodge, shortly before Marilyn Monroe's death. How Sinatra and his cronies had used Marilyn, callously encouraging her drinking and drugging, and, in DiMaggio's opinion, contributing to her death. Uncle Jim knew, long before it was common knowledge, of the affair between Monroe and JFK, and that she was shoved off onto Bobby.

"Whoremongers," he called them.

Five years later, when Bobby Kennedy lost his life to an assassin's bullet, Uncle Jim's comment was, "Good. The bastard got what he deserved."

Robert Kennedy had been a thorn in my uncle's side ever since his appointment by his brother as Attorney General. Later in his life, he would have more to say about the Kennedys and the events surrounding the election of JFK. As each of the Kennedy assassinations assailed the nation, Uncle Jim expressed great joy and said, simply, "I wish I could have pulled the trigger myself."

BANJO

My father was the only one who ever spoke openly to me about Uncle Jim's life and the underworld. Daddy was in it but not of it. He was just a hustler trying to make a buck, and he always did. But it could be dangerous. "Think of it like being in the army," he told me. If you wanted to participate, you had to deal with the violence.

Once, Daddy loaned his car to a couple of guys who used it to do a holdup during which somebody got killed. He got a call asking him to meet them at such and such hotel, but he had already been tipped that they were planning to knock him off because his car linked them to the ill-fated robbery. Daddy told them, "Sure, I'll be right over." Then, he packed a bag and left for Florida, where he stayed until the heat was off.

He had a partner that he referred to as "the Greek" and they would scream horribly at each other over the phone. Daddy said if you had a Greek as a friend you didn't need an enemy.

I had never really spent much time with my father. I knew him more through the eyes of others. To my mother, he was a meal ticket, which is what he sometimes called me. To my uncle and aunt, he was a buffoon with a loud voice and crude manners.

By the mid-Sixties, my marriage to Bill had produced two children and ended in divorce. Uncle Jim took on the job of supporting me and my kids, and I made a deal with my father. I would move into the Central Park West apartment with the stipulation that he could stay there whenever he was in New York.

To me, he had a bit of the sad tramp about him. A Chaplinesque quality that was touching. He was a clever, detached, lonely survivor. Agreeing to share an apartment provided a long overdue opportunity to get to know him.

He told me about one of his sisters who was struggling financially back in the Forties. He offered to take one of her twins off her hands, but his sister set him straight.

"Nobody is taking any of my kids, Benny. And, you're gonna' be sorry, someday, that you let your brother-in-law have *your* kid."

He always pulled a handkerchief out of his jacket pocket and wiped his eyes unashamedly when he repeated this.

When he talked about making a will and leaving whatever he had to my kids, I was outraged. "Are you going to pass me by, like you passed on the chance to be a father?"

To the end of his life, worldly possessions meant nothing to him. When he died, he left a suitcase with a few articles of clothing and a cigar box that contained some dice, a photograph of my mother, and an official schedule for the Clyde Beatty-Cole Bros. Circus for 1973.

Also in the cigar box were two sheets of paper containing a cryptic list of names, among them: Sneeze Mob, Young Zulu Kid, Arnold Rothstein, The Dancer, Long George, Fats Manning, Charlton Heston, Cecil B. DeMille, Gloria Graham, Virginia Graham, Chris Dundee, Frank Erickson, John North, Johnny Dunn, Matt & Frank Gentile.

I have never been able to come up with a reasonable explanation.

Daddy was a terrific raconteur. His story about trying to kill Hitler (or, rather, not trying to kill him) was amazing. As were his stories about the circus.

For twenty years, he traveled every season with the Ringling Brothers, Barnum & Bailey Circus, where he ran the crap game for the employees. It seemed very interesting to me that he did this. He took great delight in bringing every kid he knew—me, my friends, his nieces and nephews—to see the circus. This was his gift.

He spoke about the elephants, how intelligent they were and that they had their own pets. He saw elephants become very despondent after the death of a pet dog or cat. He marveled at the way the children of the circus folk ran around amidst the working elephants and all the activity—and never seemed to get hurt. He said that, of all the nationalities he dealt with at the circus, the Japanese were the most honorable. If a Japanese man owed you a dime, he would walk twenty miles to pay you back.

There was a story he liked to tell about a time when John Ringling North came to him with a problem. Gangs of roughnecks had been following the circus and robbing the clientele.

"Banjo, can you do something about these bastards?" Mr. North asked.

"Don't worry," my father told him, "I'll take care of it."

Daddy wasn't a tough guy like Uncle Jim. But he had major street smarts. He enlisted a few of the roustabouts from the circus and supplied them with pistols. He instructed them to hide at strategic spots, that night, after the show. On his signal, they were to fire the pistols into the air and run around, shouting and making an impressive racket. In the midst of all the chaos, my father recognized the leader of this motley crew of thieves and grabbed the man by his collar. Using the foulest language he could come up with, he threatened him with death if he ever showed his face around the circus again.

Mission accomplished.

Every year, on my birthday, my father gave me a piece of diamond jewelry; but the best gift I ever got from him was a ride on an elephant. For years, Daddy had been asking me if I'd like to ride an elephant in the circus parade. Finally, when I was about twenty, I answered, "Hey. Put your money where your mouth is!" And he did.

Several weeks later, Mary Lee and I were introduced by the ringmaster as a couple of Hollywood starlets and out we came, riding atop two huge elephants at the front of the parade. Now, how many people can say they've done that?

When I was a little girl, Daddy used to say he was going to write a book about me and call it *How Carole Came Home in a Barrel*. He was always going to teach me a song called *"No Sleeves in Papa's Vest."* He would often break out into pig Latin, starting off with, "You see, kid, you have to understand the elements of psychology," and the rest descended into crazy double-talk. This went along with the sleight-of-hand card tricks that he excelled at and the turtles, lizards and snakes that he habitually brought home.

AFTER MY DIVORCE from Bill Stephens in the early sixties, the years that I lived in my parents' Central Park West apartment with my two small children, Sean and Laurel, were some of the happiest of my life. The children provided me with a job that made me feel good about myself. As good as I could feel, that is. I still suffered with bouts of depression and spent time in bed with the covers pulled over my head. Some days, I found it impossible to go outside. Luckily, Uncle Jim paid for a nanny to help me.

I brought my mother and the children with me when I got a job as a go-go girl and danced in a cage at a beachside club in Atlantic City, where I was billed as Miss Hullabaloo, after a popular television show. I became a bit of a local celebrity with a life-size cutout of myself perched on the top of the building. It was in that dilapidated town featuring sun, surf and a generous assortment of young would-be wise guys that I met a handsome bartender named Joe Russo. He was a cross between Richard Burton and Sean Connery and who could resist that? When I left Atlantic City at the end of the summer, Joe came with me.

Joe Russo

When Daddy met my boyfriend (who was soon to become my second and final husband), he was suspicious. He confronted Joe, a man of few words, who said, "But, Mr. Contrada, I love your daughter."

"I'd love her, too, if I were you," was his reply. In his mind, it was all about Uncle Jim. After all, who wouldn't want to marry the niece of Jimmy Blue Eyes?

JOE and I married and I gave birth to a son we named Kevin. With two school-aged children, a baby and a husband who didn't share my love of Manhattan, I allowed myself to be persuaded to relocate. Uncle Jim had connections in Las Vegas and South Florida. Which did we prefer? Since wild horses couldn't have forced me to move to Vegas—Florida it was!

With a down payment from my uncle, we bought a house in Miami where Joe got a job. When the dust settled and I began to contemplate my life and what I had done with it, I brooded. I cried. Not only had I given up my beloved apartment, I had given up all of New York; and worst of all, I had given up my dreams. I went crazy. I got on my knees and began pulling weeds out of the grass.

Joe called my uncle and aunt. "You'd better come over here," he said. "Carole is sitting in a chair, just staring into space."

When they arrived, they were somber. They talked about me as if I wasn't there. "We'd better get a psychiatrist," they said.

I felt dead inside. Nothing to live for. I had dug myself into a deep hole that I couldn't get out of.

Carole, miserable in Miami, with Joe, Flo & Jimmy

After months of therapy, I slowly began to accept my situation and find a way to somehow build a new life. I had no other choice. Daddy's doctor called me from the Veteran's Hospital in New Jersey to say that my father had lung cancer and had six months to live. Then Daddy got on the phone.

"Don't tell your mother," he whispered, protective of her to the end.

Naturally, I told her immediately. A month later, she collapsed as she opened the front door of her house. Her two dogs, romping around the street, alerted a neighbor, who called me. A brain scan revealed a tumor.

My mother was pretty much gone after the operation. Meyer got her into Mt. Sinai for radiation treatments. When her hair grew in, it was the most shimmering shade of silver.

"Would you like to see Daddy?" I would ask her.

"Not today. Maybe next week," she would say.

Daddy didn't push it. Every day, he went to the hospital and stood in the hall, outside my mother's room. He never saw her alive again. Six months after my mother died, Daddy passed on too. The strange thing is, after all the turmoil and all the pain, I don't think either one of them wanted to exist without the other.

I lost both my parents at the age of twenty-nine; but in a sense, I had already lost them years before. In the end, I think my mother was right. My uncle and aunt stole me. They stole my affection. They stole my respect. On the other hand, didn't my father and mother give me away? Didn't they abdicate their position as parents? They must have thought they could get me back at some later, more convenient time, as if they had loaned my uncle and aunt an article of clothing or a piece of furniture.

WHEN MY FATHER and mother died within six months of each other, Uncle Jim had been convicted of obstruction of justice and was serving time in Atlanta State Penitentiary. He instructed Aunty Doe to take care of the funeral expenses of both my parents.

WHO KILLED GEORGE WOOD?

A gadget called Scopitone was about to cause big trouble for Jimmy Blue Eyes. A cross between a jukebox and a twenty-six inch color TV, Scopitone originated in France and was the ancestor of today's music video. In the early Sixties, George Wood brought it to America, under the auspices of the William Morris Agency. A company was formed and stock was distributed among a group of partners. At roughly the same time that Scopitone was being developed, Uncle Jim met a Miami Beach attorney named Alvin Malnik.

Malnik was smitten with celebrity mobsters. When he met Jimmy Blue Eyes, he hit the jackpot. With Uncle Jim, flattery could get you somewhere and Malnik was smooth. Uncle Jim took Al under his wing and introduced him around. Al was a mover and he soon accumulated various businesses and a substantial fortune. Uncle Jim introduced Malnik to George Wood and that's how he wound up as a controlling partner in Scopitone.

By 1962 the government was associating Malnik with top organized crime figures. Their suspicions led them to envision a link between Malnik and Meyer Lansky. It was rumored that Malnik was Meyer's attorney and possibly his heir apparent. To those interested in weaving theoretical webs, Malnik, being a short Jewish man, seemed to be perfectly cast as Meyer's understudy.

"Al never even knew Meyer," Uncle Jim later told me. "They happened to ride in the same elevator together, one day. The rest is bullshit."

IN THE LATE FIFTIES, the New York District Attorney's Office was illegally wire-tapping George Wood's office on the 20th Floor of the Mutual Life Building. They'd stumbled across George in the course of a boxing investigation and, while monitoring his conversations, they discovered his connections to the mob.

George Wood & Jimmy

With his street smarts and winning personality, George was the perfect conduit between the guys who owned the joints and those who were looking to work in them. He knew everybody, including the big wheels in the underworld. To the detectives investigating organized crime in the Manhattan's district attorney's office, George's connections seemed ominous. They were so anxious to pin something on him that they even reported that he was "once married to Meyer Lansky's sister." That would have been news to Meyer's sister, Esther, who didn't even know George.

The D.A.'s office envisioned a scenario in which the underworld was in control of the entertainment industry, and George was right at the heart of it. A kind of conspiracy theory emerged, in which the roster of talent represented by the William Morris Agency (entertainers such as Jimmy Durante, Joe E. Lewis, Carmen Miranda, and all the headliners who had appeared at the Colonial Inn) were actually *managed by the mob*. In the theatrical business, there was nothing unique about having relationships and making connections. But the notion that just by knowing the right people, and putting those people together, wheels could be oiled and deals could be made, didn't fit in with the picture the boys in the district attorney's office were trying to paint. It was too simple to be true.

Frank Hogan was New York's racket busting district attorney in 1961. Dewey had created a group of handpicked men dedicated to fighting organized crime. He assigned twenty-five year old Detective Robert Nicholson the task of monitoring the taped conversations from George Wood's office phone.

Nicholson, a squeaky-clean rookie, had no experience with the Meyer Lanskys, Jimmy Blue Eyes, or, for that matter, the George Woods of the world. To put it simply, he was a "square" with comic book impressions of the inner workings of organized crime.

Not long after Hogan ordered Nicholson to dig up information on George, Hal Roach, Jr., son of the Hollywood producer of the

Harold Lloyd and Laurel and Hardy films, reported to the Manhattan DA's office that organized crime figures seemed to be involved in the Scopitone deal, for which he had recently been hired to make films.

Nicholson, showing remarkable ingenuity, managed to gain entry to George's office and plant a microphone under a leather armchair so he was able to pick up, not only phone conversations, but anything said by people who dropped by George's office, such as Jimmy Blue Eyes, Frank Costello, and Roy Cohn. He also discovered that George was cozy with a couple of agents from the FBI's New York office and that he often provided them with girls and sent them off to be wined and dined at upscale night spots.

Nicholson thought he had hit the mother lode. All of his findings were reported to J. Edgar Hoover who, evidently, couldn't care less. So he cooked up a plot. His hope was that he could turn George into an informant by threatening him with jail time. His golden opportunity presented itself when he overheard Jimmy Blue Eyes asking George to go to Naples to meet with Lucky Luciano. George was to retrieve certain financial papers that were needed to resolve a business deal between Luciano, who would die months later, and someone in the States.

George arranged to deliver the paperwork to Uncle Jim at Rumplemeyer's Restaurant on the night of his arrival home. From Italy, he contacted his two FBI pals and asked them to pick him up at the airport and escort him through customs. This threw a monkey wrench into Nicholson's plan to arrest George at the airport. He must have been furious when he realized he wasn't going to be able to confiscate the papers George was carrying and threaten him with jail time—a fate he would surely agree to avoid by becoming a "stoolie" for the D.A.'s office.

ME AND JIMMY BLUE EYES

Not long after that fiasco, Nicholson overheard the two FBI agents tell George they'd been assigned to tail Jimmy Blue Eyes. They asked George if he could make their job easier by alerting them when his friend was in town. Nicholson's boss, Frank Hogan, having enough of this business of FBI agents playing footsies with a known associate of gangsters, went to Washington to confront J. Edgar Hoover. Hoover, in turn, sent word to the agents about Hogan's charges against them. The two agents, Frick and Frack, unaware of the bug underneath the armchair, immediately rushed to George's office and told him that his phone was bugged!

The next day, Hoover was informed that his agents had committed a serious crime and they were unceremoniously dumped from the agency.

NICHOLSON WAS TAILING George on a Friday night in early November, as he strolled over to the Camelot Supper Club on East Forty-Ninth Street. The place was a hangout where wise guys could often be found having a drink at the bar. Nicholson stayed outside, waiting to see what might develop. After a short time, he decided to enter the club; and as did, he passed a couple of bouncers carrying out a man whose face was covered with a bloody towel. Inside, Nicholson discovered, to his surprise, that George was nowhere in sight. The following Monday morning, via the taped conversation from George's office, he heard that George had suffered a massive coronary over the weekend—and was dead.

In fact, the person being carried out of the Camelot that Friday night was George, who had experienced a blackout and fallen, bloodying his face. The next morning, he went to his doctor at Mount Sinai Hospital for a cardiogram. As he was telling the doctor a joke, and before he got to the punch line, he had a heart attack and fell over dead. A few days later, at Campbell's Funeral Home, the same mix of show biz and the underworld who had populated his life attended the funeral ceremony. Everyone from Ed Sullivan and Tallulah Bankhead to Frank Costello showed up.

George Jessel delivered the eulogy. From where I was seated with my uncle and aunt, I wondered if I were the only one fascinated by the droop of Jessel's hopelessly crooked toupee. Down the hall, Elsa Maxwell, the well-known social climber and party giver, was laid out and Aunty Doe whispered what a shame it was that nobody seemed to be showing up for Maxwell's final bash.

The place was jammed with people from all corners of the entertainment industry, and I have no doubt that Detective Nicholson was lurking somewhere in the room that day, mingling with the crowd.

As astonishing as it seems, Nicholson and the other "Keystone Cops" in the District Attorney's office developed a theory. In their minds, George's death had, in fact, been a "hit." They reasoned that his relationship with the two FBI agents, Tracy and Hayes, meant that he was an FBI informant, passing on information about the mob. Hadn't they heard with their own ears, Jimmy Blue Eyes repeatedly warning George that his friendship with Tracy and Hayes didn't look good to "the boys?" So they cooked up a scenario in which the "commission" sent Jimmy to reason with George, but George refused to listen. That was his "death warrant!" He had to be "whacked!" Furthermore, if Jimmy wasn't capable of killing his friend, or having him killed, then he himself would be killed. According to Nicholson and Hogan—this was the code of the mob!

The truth is that no one will ever know what the relationship between George Wood and the agents, Tracy and Hayes, entailed. Were the two agents simply enjoying the perks of hanging around the fabulous theatrical agent who could turn them on to starlets and provide them entrée to café society hangouts? Was he keeping the agents around just for laughs? Was George an informant? If so, why?

Talking about it years later, Uncle Jim scoffed at the bizarre story, saying, "It's ridiculous. I was the godfather to his daughter, for Christ's sake. The best man at his wedding. I was his best friend."

What we do know is that George, most assuredly, was not murdered. He died at Mt. Sinai Hospital and his natural death is documented and undisputed. Once again, rumors surrounding Uncle Jim and his world flourished, unchecked by reality.

NOT ONLY DID George leave his wife, Lois, high and dry without a penny to fall back on; but also he was in hock to loan sharks up to his eyeballs. Uncle Jim intervened on Lois's behalf with the shylocks who wanted their money. He told them, "She's got nothin'. Forget about it." And they did.

Lois was desperate for money, so Uncle Jim arranged for her to go to work at the Pompeii, a swanky Park Avenue restaurant where we frequently ate. The Pompeii employed two elderly violinists who drove my uncle to such exasperation that he would wave them away as if he were chasing flies. Lois went on the payroll, and for the next several months, strolled around the room, followed by the musicians with their tinny violins. Smiling her toothy smile, she sang show tunes while the customers were free to ignore her or politely pause to listen between bites of lobster or filet mignon. As it happened, fate was waiting in the wings for Lois. One night, as she was serenading, she caught the attention of Generoso Pope, Jr.

In 1952, Pope, with a substantial loan from his godfather, Frank Costello, had purchased a foundering publication called the *New York Inquirer*, renamed it the *National Enquirer* and fashioned it into the first major tabloid newspaper, featuring attention-grabbing stories about UFOs and three-headed dogs.

One day I visited Lois at her apartment, and surrounded by our sleeping children, we settled into the deep cushions of her living room couches for afternoon tea. Her mother was visiting—as usual—and the subject came around to Gene Pope.

"He's asked me to marry him," Lois said, "but I have reservations about his *character*." Lois and her mother tossed the subject of Pope's suitability back and forth with great seriousness. Did they think George Wood was a paragon of virtue? Not surprisingly, it didn't take long for Lois to overcome her doubts and accept Gene's proposal.

A big engagement bash was held at the Pope mansion in Westchester. I have pictures of my aunt, Billie Giné, and me sitting primly on a settee. Beside us stand the musicians from the Pompeii, wielding their violins. Uncle Jim doesn't appear in any of the pictures. Was he there? I doubt it. All I know is, we ate, we drank, we danced, we sang.

And none of us ever heard from Lois O'Brien Wood again.

One can only assume that, despite the shady reputation of his own godfather, Frank Costello, Gene Pope was not interested in having any connection to Jimmy Blue Eyes. I often heard my uncle say, "There's nothing worse than an ingrate." It was part of his nature to help people out—but he expected a little gratitude in return. He was disappointed many times in his life—but in the case of Lois Wood, it cut deeply.

When she married Gene Pope, she moved into a different stratum of society—and took her place at the head of a long line of ingrates in Uncle Jim's life. He had loved George and extended much of that same affection to Lois. She enchanted him with her smile, her beauty, her apparent graciousness, and she betrayed him.

Like Uncle Jim himself, she proved to have another face.

COOKED UP

It had been twenty years since Ben Siegel had envisioned the Flamingo Hotel, which would lead to the shimmering mecca Las Vegas was to become. In 1967 Howard Hughes began to buy up the major hotels on the Vegas strip. The first was the Desert Inn. Then he bought the Sands from Jack Entratter and the other partners (those who could be named). It was the end of an era of gritty, sexy glamour—with a little bit of danger on the side. The hey-day of "the mob" was over in Vegas.

Uncle Jim couldn't care less. He said to Meyer, "We're getting old. Let's take the money and lead a quiet life."

But it wasn't to be.

The Indictment

THE FEDS HAD BEEN GUNNING for Uncle Jim for years. In May of 1966, he answered a subpoena to appear before the Securities and

Exchange Commission investigating Scopitone. He suspected a perjury trap. Rather than taking the Fifth Amendment, he told the truth about the meetings he had attended at the Warwick Hotel to settle a dispute between a group of Scopitone investors.

He didn't tell the committee how Al Malnik, who owned a controlling percentage of the company, had sought him out in Italy, where he was vacationing with my aunt. He didn't tell them, as he later told me:

> I was gettin' out of a taxi in front of the hotel and there's Al standin' there. Jesus Christ, I was stupefied! He runs up to me and says, "Jimmy, I need your help." So we take a walk and he tells me his Scopitone partners are threatenin' to kill him. When I get back to the States, I have a couple of meetings with these guys to straighten things out. But they were madder than hell and didn't want to listen. So I washed my hands of it. These guys were nothin'. They were just businessmen. They wouldn't kill a cockroach. But they threatened. I couldn't tell the committee that.

Uncle Jim answered the committee as honestly as he could. To many questions he said, "I don't recall."

Three years went by. Nothing happened. But unbeknownst to Uncle Jim, the matter was far from over. As he would later repeat again and again, "They were cookin' me up."

And cook him up, they did.

In 1969 Robert Morganthau, US Attorney for the Southern District of New York, brought an indictment against Vincent Alo, AKA Jimmy Blue Eyes, on a charge of Obstruction of Justice. Uncle Jim pleaded "not guilty." After three years, his testimony before the SEC was coming back to haunt him.

On January 23, 1970, Jimmy appeared before the Joint Legislative Commission of Crime. More cautious this time around, he invoked the Fifth Amendment on all questions. When he was asked about the color of his eyes (he wore tinted glasses throughout his entire testimony), he took the Fifth on that too. It got a big laugh.

Barry Slotnick, the attorney who would handle Uncle Jim's appeals, believed that Al Malnik was the true target of the government's Scopitone investigation—and that, unable to nail *him*, they turned to Jimmy Blue Eyes, the man with the shady reputation and the catchy name.

The case hinged on the illegal wiretaps on Malnik's office phones, three years previously. The government's *theory* about Malnik was that he was an important figure in the *international crime syndicate* and an intimate of Meyer Lansky. But they had no proof.

They suspected Malnik of receiving skimmed money from Las Vegas. In 1963 Attorney General Robert Kennedy gave the go-ahead to use electronic surveillance in order to move the investigation forward. Kennedy would later deny that he had authorized the illegal wiretaps, instead, placing the blame on the FBI.

The wiretapping of Malnik's office *tainted* the entire case. First, because he had no criminal record, but, more importantly, *because he was an attorney*. Therefore, the case, along with Jimmy's 1966 indictment, had to be suppressed. During Jimmy's trial in 1970, his attorney, Jay Goldberg, would argue that his civil liberties had been violated due to the fact that he had been denied a speedy trial which he was entitled to under the law.

Uncle Jim's problem was his 1966 SEC testimony. He should have taken the Fifth Amendment. Instead, in two days of testimony, he answered four hundred questions concerning the meeting at the Warwick Hotel.

One hundred sixty-two questions, he answered fully. To one hundred nineteen, he answered, "Yes" or "No." The other one hundred eleven questions he would later call, "Bullshit" or "Ham sandwich questions," as in, "What did you have for lunch?"

Then there was that one question that elicited his oft-quoted statement, "To the best of my recollection . . . I don't remember!"

When he testified that he couldn't remember the color of the drapes in the hotel room, he was accused of being "evasive." His mistake was answering questions and co-operating with a court that was clearly out to get him.

The 1966 indictment wasn't pursued because it was based on *illegal wiretapping* of Malnik's office. The government claimed that the voice of Jimmy Blue Eyes, which would have served to exonerate him, was never heard on the tapes. The transcripts of the surveillance logs were suppressed in the court hearings and the information never made available for Uncle Jim's defense.

As for Malnik himself, he did nothing to prevent what was happening to my uncle. He took the Fifth when he was questioned by the grand jury. He failed to testify on Uncle Jim's behalf. He submitted no affidavits or letters to help clear the person whose help he had begged for in Italy.

This is how Uncle Jim was repaid for his efforts.

The Trial

UNCLE JIM'S trial was presided over by Judge Constance Baker Motley. It must have galled him to submit to the authority of a woman—and a black woman, at that. It had always infuriated me that in spite of Uncle Jim's kindness toward and even affection for our dear Hattie, he had never considered her an equal.

Judge Motley graduated from Columbia Law School and was among those who stood on the podium when Martin Luther King, Jr., delivered his "I Have a Dream" speech. She was an accomplished and formidable woman. Uncle Jim was not amused.

With his flamboyant attorney, Jay Goldberg, by his side, Jimmy sat silently in the summer heat, as large fans moved the stuffy air around. He had a hunch that Motley would prove to be a "government judge." But Goldberg, knowing Judge Motley to be a staunch advocate for civil rights, believed they would benefit from trying the case before her.

In his opening statement, Goldberg, in his deep, melodious voice, explained to the jury that transcripts of Jimmy's SEC testimony would show he answered the questions honestly and to the best of his ability. He didn't hide behind the Fifth Amendment and he met with the principals involved in the division of Scopitone stock simply as a mediator. Goldberg promised that Malnik (seated at the back of the courtroom on the first day) would testify in Jimmy's defense.

The prosecutors were Gary Naftalis, a youthful and idealistic Assistant U.S. Attorney and Assistant U.S. Attorney Givens, who, during the SEC interrogation three years earlier, had posed the question: "How many people have you killed?" With no hesitation, Uncle Jim replied, "I was never in the army." Bullseye!

It was crime-busting time, courtroom drama, cops and robbers all the way. But it had its comic elements. When Naftalis stiffly read

Jimmy's quirky answers from the SEC transcripts, there were snickers throughout the courtroom.

The prosecution believed that Jimmy was an "undisclosed principal," in the SEC's Scopitone investigation, but that wasn't supposed to be the issue. They needed to pin *something* on him. They would have liked to bring perjury charges—but it would have been impossible to prove, since that necessitates getting into someone's head when they say they don't remember. They settled on Obstruction of Justice and accused Jimmy of being *evasive* and *contemptuous of the court*. I can just imagine how hard it must have been for Uncle Jim to *hide* his contempt.

On the first day, the prosecution called their star witnesses: Morris Uchitel, Alfred Miniaci, Irving Kaye, and Abe Green. All testified that the meeting at the Warwick had been friendly and attorneys eventually handled the matter. They all gave evasive answers and had trouble remembering what had actually happened at the Warwick. They were never charged with anything.

It was during Miniaci's testimony that Naftalis achieved one of his major goals. It had been previously ruled that the government could not bring the alias, "Jimmy Blue Eyes" into the indictment because it was too prejudicial. But now, because it emerged as part of the grand jury testimony, Naftalis wanted to read it into the record. Goldberg objected and told Judge Motley if this was done, he would move for a mistrial. In the judge's chambers, the prosecutor and defense attorney duked it out. Goldberg argued that the inclusion of that nickname would "strip him of his dignity."

To which, Motley replied, "I don't think so because it doesn't indicate why he is known as Blue Eyes . . . the man may be known as Jimmy Blue Eyes because he had blue eyes . . . how is that prejudicial? Blue eyes are regarded as something beautiful in this society. Why is that prejudicial to have blue eyes?"

The sarcasm and racial overtone of the remark is obvious. All Goldberg could say was, "At least Jimmy Blue Eyes is not as bad as Machine Gun Kelly."

Maybe so, but the inclusion of the alias sent a message loud and clear to the jury that the man who sat before them in the courtroom with his cigar-store-Indian face, his tinted glasses, his expensive sport coat was... Organized Crime. Regardless of the facts, now the case was tainted. On top of that, Naftalis took every opportunity to insinuate that Vincent Alo, alias Jimmy Blue Eyes, was a "man to be feared."

Goldberg called one defense witness, attorney Henry Chapman, who had represented Jimmy in 1966, when he appeared before the SEC. It was he who had advised Jimmy to answer honestly what he could—and, as for what he could not remember, to say so. He testified to this and said that he had never expected his client to be indicted on Obstruction of Justice charges.

Goldberg never called Alvin Malnik to the stand. In his closing argument, he maintained there was no proof whatsoever that his client had attempted to lie to the SEC. Raising his voice dramatically, he declared, "The lack of evidence in the case demands an acquittal!"

Prosecutor Naftalis countered with the parable of King Solomon. He said that this Vincent Alo had been called in like Solomon to decide between two factions—but that Jimmy was not a *Wise man*, only a *Wise guy*. "Who is this Vincent Alo? This Solomon?" he asked the court.

The jury retired to deliberate at 12:35 p.m. By 7:00 p.m., they delivered the verdict: guilty on two counts of Obstruction of Justice.

Uncle Jim and his council were in shock.

At the sentencing, Goldberg appealed to Judge Motley for leniency, stating that Jimmy was a family man who had been married for forty years, had no criminal record, and posed no threat to the community. In rebuttal, Naftalis pointed out that Joseph Valachi (apparently, the government's official authority on the subject) had named Vincent Alo as a high-ranking official in the Vito Genovese Mafia family.

Judge Motley gave the defendant an opportunity to make a statement.

"Well, your honor," Uncle Jim answered quietly, "I tried to cooperate with the government, but in the twenty months that elapsed between the hearing and the meeting there were some things that I just couldn't remember."

At that point, Judge Motley asked Jimmy what was his occupation —to which he answered, "None at all at this time."

With that, Motley announced that Jimmy be sentenced to a term of five years. Naftalis argued that Jimmy was a flight risk. He further asserted that Jimmy posed a danger to the witnesses and to the community.

Indignant, Goldberg brushed that statement aside and went on to make his points: "The defendant was denied his right to a speedy trial. He was indicted in 1966 and the government buried that indictment." He stated there would be an appeal.

The judge countered that there would be *no bail*, pending appeal. She remanded Jimmy to jail.

"This is an outrage," Goldberg yelled. "I can't see why he has got to sit in jail while this case is prosecuted by way of appeal. If anybody obstructed justice in this case, it's the United States Attorney," referring to Robert Morganthau, who oversaw the indictments in 1966 and 1969.

At this point, Naftalis brought up Jimmy's long-since expunged 1923 armed robbery charge. Goldberg protested angrily and there was a ruckus in the judge's chambers.

Judge Motley abruptly ended the proceedings.

"Is the United States marshal here?" she asked in a commanding tone. "Will you please take the defendant?"

As Uncle Jim was led away in handcuffs, Goldberg jumped to his feet and addressed the judge.

"Most respectfully, I want the record to reflect, from the time I started this case, I have been treated in a way in which I have never been treated by any court."

Motley shot back, "I think, in a minute, we are going to have a lawyer in jail for contempt of court—that is what I think."

Uncle Jim was taken to the Federal Detention Headquarters, commonly known as West Street Jail. He was held there for three months until he was moved to Atlanta State Prison, where he would spend the next three years.

Thirty years later, at the end of the Millennium, Uncle Jim had this to say about his trial and the treatment he received at the hands of the federal government:

Bobby Kennedy sicced Morganthau onto me. Morganthau was in it up to his elbows—but he knew he had a bull by the horns. He didn't want Al to go on trial, didn't want to be caught tapping a lawyer's phone. But he wanted to do Kennedy's bidding. So he suppressed the whole thing for three years. We didn't know any of this, at the time. We had no access to any of this information. The government denied that my voice was on those illegal tapes. Jay Goldberg wanted to call Al as a witness, but I said, "No." I didn't want to jeopardize the kid. I didn't know the government wanted to suppress those tapes.

Besides, I wasn't worried because my lawyers thought the case was nothin'. The Obstruction of Justice indictment from 1966 was suppressed in the Southern District of New York. The information would have proved I was denied a speedy trial. We found out later. By then I had done my time.

Why didn't they indict those other guys, Miniaci, Kaye, Green, and Uchitel? Because they wanted me, that's why. On top of everything else, Motley met with Naftalis a week before the trial. That's ex parte communication. It's illegal. That prick, Naftalis, was Morganthau's man. He was on a vendetta against me. By the time he got through, he had the jury believing I shot Lincoln.

The funny thing is, even though Jay lost my case, he attributes his future success to me. He got known. That's what he told me. He never forgot about me. Always wrote me encouraging letters while I was away. I got no beef with him, he did his best. But they cooked me up. If they could of gotten me for spittin' on the sidewalk, that's what they would have done."

For the rest of his life, Uncle Jim would ruminate over what had happened to him at the age of sixty-six. He'd explain to anyone listening the way the authorities bent the rules in order to "get him"—because he was a target. Organized Crime. The Justice Department is supposed to prosecute crimes, not target individuals. They didn't play fair.

"Do I have to pay forever," he asked, "for the sins of my youth?"

On the other hand, it never seemed to occur to him that he had gotten away with a lifetime of illegal activities and prospered greatly as a result.

DOING TIME

Uncle Jim turned out to be as popular in prison as he was on the outside. His reputation preceded him and brought him respect from the general population. He worked in the prison library, read books, studied Spanish, and counseled fellow inmates in whatever ways he could.

He wrote chatty, affectionate letters to my aunt—never failing to enquire about the health and wellbeing of close friends and all of us in the family. He was as interested as ever in the events of the day and pithy comments filled his letters. It's hard to miss the irony of my uncle's situation as he sat behind bars on trumped up charges and watched as Nixon and his felonious cronies were dragged through the mud.

Letter of May 12, 1973

Dear Flo,

I've been watching TV on the Watergate hearings. [John] Dean has been on all week and he is doing a pretty good job of burying those Nazis. It couldn't happen to a nicer bunch of guys. Law and order went out the window as far as they were concerned. Well, we will wait and see what happens. Oh! I forgot to tell you, I took the high school test . . . if I pass I will get twenty-five dollars. Great, isn't it?

Letter of June 29, 1973

Dear Flo,

Today it rained. I am thinking of the Ellsburg case. The judge acquitted and threw the case out, on account of the government's misconduct . . . At least Mitchell and the rest of them are in hot water. I wonder how they like it. They are the people who want to put everybody in jail. It looks like the chickens came home to roost. Well, the heck with them—let's think about ourselves.

Uncle Jim enjoyed the many encouraging cards and letters he received from friends and family.

He even corresponded with the film star Silvana Mangano, whom he had met in Italy with her husband, film producer, Dino DeLaurentis. As a man who always appreciated a good-looking woman, it must have pleased my uncle to receive letters written by the gorgeous and gracious Mangano. They were written in Italian and Uncle Jim had another inmate read them and help him reply.

On December 20, 1973, his last day—Uncle Jim was taken to a holding room, and those who wanted to were allowed to come and say goodbye. The room filled up with blacks, whites, and Hispanics. Young and Old. They all hugged him and wished him well. As he later remembered it, "For a minute there, I didn't wanna leave!"

Although he would always feel a seething resentment about what had happened to him, Uncle Jim emerged from prison relatively unscathed. Aunty Doe passed through the ordeal with her usual fortitude. Being the tough cookies that they were, it seemed they could take anything life could dish out. But there was more to come.

Uncle Jim was sixty-nine years old when he came out of Atlanta. He had done the time *standing on his head*, as they say. On the day of his release, my aunt, who had traveled to Atlanta to visit him constantly during the three years of his prison term, was waiting to accompany him home to New York.

THROUGHOUT THE SEVENTIES, Uncle Jim's character was sorely tried. He had led a charmed life; but no one gets through without paying some dues, and, my uncle, unassailable though he seemed, was paying his.

After Atlanta, the family was assailed by a series of tragedies, beginning with the death of one of my aunt's grandsons. Little Larry had been battling leukemia for several years. When Uncle Jim called from Las Vegas to say that the sixteen-year-old boy had passed away, hearing his voice crack over the phone was heartbreaking. Although I knew he cared deeply about the grandchildren, it was hard for me to picture my hardboiled uncle with tears in his eyes.

Little Larry's sweet and gentle mother, Franny, spiraled into a deep depression after the loss of her middle son. Lying beside the swimming pool, she somehow slipped into the water and drowned. Years later Uncle Jim would tell me he believed Franny's death had been a suicide.

Not long after that, my aunt's other daughter-in-law—Billy's wife, Judy—took her own life. She had suffered from depression since childhood. After sending my cousin and their two children out for burgers, Judy lay down in bed and shot herself. Billy, whose luck just never seemed to hold out, would be struck down by cancer several years later.

Uncle Jim and Aunty Doe, the great survivors, managed to withstand these blows with their usual stoicism. I cannot recall seeing my aunt ever shed a tear or show any other indication of vulnerability. Where they both were stuffing their emotions, I will never know.

My uncle and aunt did a lot of traveling in their later years. During the Sixties, they made yearly trips to Europe. Before his conviction, my aunt and uncle, along with a group of friends, rented a yacht with a crew of ten and cruised the Greek Islands. "It was the best vacation we ever had. It was beautiful. We took a tip from Onassis," Uncle Jim joked.

Greece

Greece

After he had done his time, they packed their bags and headed for Europe again. They visited London, where Dino Cellini had been overseeing the posh Colony Club Casino with Forties matinee idol George Raft as front man. From there they visited Italy and Israel and spent time in Amsterdam, where Uncle Jim had an interest in several casinos.

It was a time of renewal for my uncle who possessed an enormous degree of resiliency and was able to capture his joie de vivre without much effort.

THE YEAR that Uncle Jim was sent to Atlanta, one of the most successful films in the history of Hollywood, Frances Ford Coppola's *The Godfather*, was released. In my teens, I had worked as an extra on one of Coppola's first films, *You're a Big Boy Now*. He was a big bear of a guy strolling around in Bermuda shorts and he picked me out of the crowd to walk up the street with several of the principal actors. Unfortunately, it didn't increase my pay grade, but I was thrilled.

Coppola cast Marlon Brando in the title role and it seemed to me that Brando, through his innate genius, captured the quality of quiet command that I saw in Uncle Jim. Together with the under slung jaw and throaty voice, I could hardly believe that he hadn't been a fly on the wall somewhere, observing my uncle in order to come up with the mob character that he invented with uncanny accuracy.

It's rumored that the making of *The Godfather* had to be "okayed" by "the mob." I remember Uncle Jim saying that an emissary from Hollywood actually came to him to get an okay, to which he agreed, with tongue in cheek.

In 1974 *Godfather II* was released. It contained a scene in Havana, in which Lee Strasberg portrays Meyer Lansky, thinly disguised as a character named Hyman Roth. Always in the background, but never far away is the shadowy character of Johnny Ola, Hyman Roth's closest and constant companion. Ola is, obviously, Jimmy Blue Eyes. Nobody thought "permission" was needed from Meyer or Jimmy. The names were changed to protect the

studio. But they needn't have bothered.

UNCLE JIM WATCHED the *Godfather* movies on TV and got a kick out of them. I never heard him mention Johnny Ola. I suppose it might be difficult to recognize a fictionalized Hollywood version of one's self—so, it's possible the whole thing just went right over my uncle's head.

WHILE UNCLE JIM WAS AWAY, in "college," Meyer moved to Israel. Two years later, he was rejected by the land of his ancestors. Wanting to become a citizen of Israel, he asked for permanent citizenship under the Law of Return, by which any Jew has the right to find sanctuary in Zion. But Meyer's reputation got in the way. Over the years, untruths and semi-truths had been relentlessly spawned by journalists about Meyer's activities, his alleged wealth, and his power. The Israeli government became convinced that Meyer, this sickly seventy-year-old man who had been living inconspicuously among them for two years, was a dangerous character and a threat to society.

When the Israeli Supreme Court refused Meyer's request, he embarked on an odyssey that took him from Tel Aviv through Zurich to Rio to Buenos Aires to Paraguay—where he hoped to find a safe haven.

Throughout the journey, Meyer was extremely stressed and was quietly slipping nitroglycerin pills under his tongue. With the FBI monitoring his every move, he arrived in Asuncion, Paraguay, where he was denied entry and forced to remain on the plane. Sick, weary, and depressed, he had no choice but to go on to Miami where federal agents walked into the first class cabin and arrested him. He was taken to FBI headquarters where he was charged with indictments which had been issued while he was in Israel involving skimming and contempt of court. After bond was posted, he went directly from the courthouse to Mount Sinai Hospital where he suffered a heart attack.

Three days after Meyer's arrest at Miami International Airport, Teddy Lansky arrived there from Tel Aviv wearing bright red lipstick and carrying the Lansky's little dog, Bruzzer. Enraged by the gaggle of reporters surrounding and harassing her, she got into a nasty altercation with a female reporter, which would make headlines. Not one to take any crap, she spit in the woman's face.

Uncle Jim never forgave the Israelis for the way they treated his pal. He also had no qualms about voicing his negative opinion of Israel's treatment of the Palestinians, which he thought was lousy. This subject was a barrel of laughs, considering that most of my uncle's pals were Jewish. But he never had a problem saying what he thought whether his friends liked it or not. Hours were spent discussing the Israeli/Palestinian question and other problems of the world, and these issues were sometimes argued hotly during daily lunches in the coffee shop of the Singapore Hotel on Miami Beach.

Like Uncle Jim had said to Meyer back in Sixty-Seven, "Let's take the money and lead a quiet life." At last, after Uncle Jim's Scopitone ordeal leading to a three-year prison sentence—and Meyer's failing health and troubles with Israel—they were in what could be called their Golden Years. They had survived the poverty and brutality of their youth. Survived the Wild West of the Twentieth Century—Prohibition. Survived the scrutiny of the government.

They had made it to retirement in one piece—and what a hell of a ride it had been.

Jake Lansky, Jimmy & Meyer Lansky

JIMMY AND FLO—LIKE HAM AND EGGS

When my youngest son went off to college in 1986, I felt it was time to fulfill a promise I had made to myself ... finally. I left my husband behind and returned to New York alone. I was forty-five years old. My uncle and aunt were in their eightieth decade. My return to New York had them more than a little puzzled, because to them, family was all important; but for the most part, they kept their opinions to themselves.

I had never reconciled myself to living in Florida. Never stopped pining for New York. It was my husband, Joe, who wanted to move. I never completely forgave him for convincing me to give up the Central Park West apartment with all its psychological history. I was married with three kids. At twenty-nine, I thought there was no hope of ever achieving the life I had envisioned for myself.

At home, I was no angel. I even surpassed my aunt in the ability to display anger.

Arguments were monumental and often ridiculous. When Joe bought an institutional-sized soup pot, I protested that we had no place to keep it. The issue escalated to the point where I ran outside with the pot filled with chicken soup and hurled it over the fence and into the street, Later, when I sheepishly tried to retrieve the pot, it was gone. Joe didn't speak to me for a week.

In my own defense, my husband gave me better reasons than oversized pots to exercise my bad temper. I realize now that I had a problem with intimacy—and our marriage was tailor-made to accommodate our respective issues. At the same time, I felt a deep need of family and home. Although I was a loner, I very much needed something to be a part of—an anchor that would prevent me from spinning off into the universe.

In time, I managed to pull myself together, entered into a serious study of acting and discovered that it was only amongst actors that I felt I belonged. I continued to work on my voice and willed myself to overcome my crippling stage fright. Over a period of twenty years, I appeared in many plays and musicals, as well as creating and performing a nightclub act. My uncle and aunt silently disapproved, taking the position that my work as a performer was irrelevant and detrimental to my status as wife and mother. Although I enjoyed many unforgettable experiences and roles onstage, they never saw any of it. However, when I portrayed Eva Peron in Evita, my uncle and aunt surprised me by showing up. They said nothing to me, not a word of praise, but I heard through the grape vine that they were shocked.

Being in New York again was thrilling. I was entering a new phase of my life—looking to put in place a crucial piece that had been missing. I moved in with my friend, Julie Morgan, was renting the bottom floor of a duplex apartment on the upper West Side. Julie was a singer, as blonde and bubbly as I was dark and intense, and we had an 'odd couple' relationship.

Living with Julie was fun, but after six months I'd had it! Our kooky landlady, who had been in the original cast of the nude extravaganza, *Oh Calcuttta*, lived on the upper floor of the duplex. Julie and I lived on the lower floor and had to share the premises with a marauding guinea pig that, one night, squeezed under my door and jumped in bed with me. This was bad enough, but when the hairy little bastard snuck into the closet and ate one of my best shoes—I knew I had to get out of there.

I moved into a tiny studio apartment in an old Third Avenue tenement. It was a three flight walk-up but it was dirt cheap—and it was all mine.

I learned to do without anything that wouldn't fit into my cramped space. Though I longed for a pet, all I could manage was an indigo Siamese fighting fish who lived in undulating solitude in a bowl on the table where I ate. It was the first time in my life I had ever lived alone and it was an epiphany.

I took a job as a saleslady at Macy's and joined an acting class taught by the esteemed actor, William Hickey. Eccentric, gravelly-voiced Hickey had recently won an Oscar for his role in the John Huston film, *Prizzi's Honor*. Bill told fascinating stories, most of which centered around his mother, or his dog who accompanied him to every class, snoozing contentedly by his master's feet. He possessed the Irish gift of gab, which made each and every one of his classes the best show in town. To be in Bill Hickey's presence was inspirational. Again and again, he told the class: "You're all stars. You just don't know it."

During the early years of what felt to me like my banishment in Florida, I considered my uncle and aunt toxic and tried to limit the amount of time spent with them. Just to be in their presence threw me back into a feeling of childish dependency that I despised in myself. However, through it all, Uncle Jim continued to contribute generously to our family in the form of extras and luxuries for my children and me.

Now, after all the years of emotional confusion, I was reconnecting with them. George Wood, Doc Rosen, Henrí Giné—all the old gang had passed away and Uncle Jim was enjoying the company of a whole new entourage. The dancers were different, but the dance remained the same.

I WAS HAVING dinner with my uncle and aunt at Patsy's, an old West Side haunt of show folk and the underworld, when Nancy Sinatra passed by our table, stopped to say "hello" and walked on. The talk at the table immediately turned to Kitty Kelly's recently published unauthorized biography of Frank Sinatra.

Kelly was known for her poison pen celebrity bios. In the book, she outlined Sinatra's womanizing and his erratic behavior and made much of his alleged ties to organized crime. A furious Sinatra launched a two million dollar lawsuit, which he later withdrew. Aunty Doe adored Sinatra and defended him that night. Uncle Jim stuck to his opinion that Sinatra was an overrated bum.

Kelly also talks about the late George Wood, and identifies George's close friend, Jimmy Blue Eyes, as a member of the Vito Genovese Mafia family. She repeats the story that I had heard back in the early Sixties, about Sinatra's suicide attempt. She says that

George was Sinatra's babysitter, and that he was "perfect for Frank because he knew all the gangsters—Meyer Lansky, Vincent "Jimmy Blue Eyes" Alo, Frank Costello—all of them!" As far as his connection to Jimmy Blue Eyes, Sinatra is quoted as saying, "I just ran into him."

According to Kelly, producer David Susskind was casually acquainted, not only with Jimmy Blue Eyes, but also with *Jimmy's mistress,* a *woman named Kris.* Supposedly, Susskind received a call from Kris, warning him "someone wanted to hurt him."

She said the *someone* was Sinatra, who was angry because Susskind had used the singer's then-wife, Mia Farrow, in a movie when he didn't want her to work. Kris said that Sinatra wanted him roughed up but was going to "...get other gangsters to do it for him. Nothing fatal. Just break an arm and a leg."

Kelly further quotes Kris as saying, "My guy says that no one touches anyone in the East without his okay and that if anyone touches you [Susskind], he won't be alive the next day. But he says that you're not to go to Las Vegas or Miami. He can't control what goes on there."

Years later I got around to reading the Sinatra biography. I could have fallen off my chair when I got to the part about Uncle Jim and Kris. Who was she? Did she even exist? How reliable were "Kris's" quotes? One columnist, at the time, scathingly referred to the book as "Kitty litter." I have to agree. Her book is one more example of unsubstantiated facts, which the likes of my uncle could do nothing about. As for Sinatra—he sued.

I'm sure that Uncle Jim read the book and my guess is that he scoffed at the section regarding himself. I sincerely hope that my aunt never read it—and that her friends had the decency to keep their mouths shut and thus shield her from ever hearing about "Kris." But I'll never know.

~

My uncle and aunt still dressed and ate out every night. Uncle Jim had his new favorite spots: Aperitivo, around the corner on Fifty-Sixth Street, Doriental on East Fifty-Sixth for Chinese and Joe and Rose in the East Forties for a good steak after a sociable drink chatting at the bar with the proprietor. At all of these places, Uncle Jim was treated royally, which was the way he liked it.

The dinner companions now were reduced to a few. The most important of which was Uncle Jim's new best friend, Sidney Stromberg the tough of the Philadelphia Strombergs. Often, the group would be joined by somebody's widow, graciously invited by Uncle Jim, who never forgot his responsibilities to friends, living or dead. As usual, nobody but Uncle Jim ever expected to put a hand in their pocket when the check arrived.

Over the next five or six years, I would spend a lot of time with my uncle and his friend, Sidney Stromberg. I was crazy about Sidney who looked a lot like Sidney Greenstreet, the old character actor from *The Maltese Falcon*. I loved to hear him tell the story about his eighteen-year incarceration for bank robbery. At night, Sidney would read Shakespeare to his cellmate, lying in the bunk below. The man would listen raptly, absorb the essence of some archetypal character and suddenly shout out, "I know dat guy!"

A member of Greenpeace and the Sierra Club, Sidney was a copious reader and self-taught intellectual and was the perfect companion in this, the last phase of my uncle's life. These two diamonds in the rough enjoyed many lively discussions and had much to say about the politics of the day and the state of the world.

"I was lucky," Uncle Jim often repeated. "I've seen the best of this country." He felt he had had the good fortune to be born into the most interesting city and at the most opportune time imaginable. At the turn of the twentieth century, there was so much virgin territory. So many trails to be blazed. So much fun to be had.

In the next few years, I would find myself privy to more and more of my uncle's uncensored memories.

My parents—those distant inhabitants of my childhood—had died and faded into the past; and with them, went the memory of the forlorn love I had once felt for my mother—as well as the quizzical interest with which I had viewed my father. It seemed as though I had lived an entirely separate lifetime since their passing. And right to the end, they were trumped by the powerful presence and resilience of my uncle and aunt.

The days when I had felt the sharp sting of my aunt's disapproval were behind me. She had forgotten her old dreams—those dreams that had long ago held me captive.

One afternoon, Aunty Doe and I were drinking coffee and chatting about a trip she had taken to Atlantic City, some years before.

"You brought the baby to see me at the Claridge Hotel, remember?"

I realized that she was referring to *my mother* bringing *me* to visit her there. Our eyes locked for a moment and a cloud passed over her face.

"You're Grace," she said, staring hard at me. "Well, I'm not crazy. You're Grace!"

A shudder went through me, but I looked away and let the moment pass.

Aunty Doe was growing old. A year previously, a brick had fallen from a Madison Avenue construction site, knocking her unconscious, and after that, the feisty woman she had always been began to vanish. Seeing her in that fragile state, my mind flashed back to the day she marched around the corner with a baseball bat to rescue my son, Shawn, from a bully. She was no longer the fierce, defended woman I had grown up with and battled. The eagle had become a dove.

Nothing much was said between my uncle and me. I had the feeling that he was in denial about the state of her health. I wondered if he'd noticed the change in her personality. But since the dissection of personalities had never been Uncle Jim's forte, I chose to leave it alone.

I marveled at the way he handled her as she became more dependent. He buttoned the blouse that she could no longer button, held her hand as they walked in the street, and answered innocuously when she asked, "Where do we live?"

Shortly after my return to New York, Aunty Doe and I went to buy airline tickets at an Eastern Airline ticket office on Fifth Avenue. It was crowded when we arrived, so we took a number and sat down to wait. Suddenly, the entrance of an older woman wearing a dramatic red cape electrified the atmosphere. She strode up to the counter and interrupted the clerk who was busy with a customer. He asked her to take a number, but she insisted on his immediate attention.

With that, my aunt spoke up. "Why don't you take a number and wait your turn, like the rest of us?"

The woman stiffened and turned. "Do you know to whom you are speaking? *I* was in *pictures*!" said the woman.

"Oh, yeah? Who were you? Rin Tin Tin?" my aunt shot back.

With that, the woman stepped forward, stood over Aunty Doe, and slapped her. The next thing I knew, my seventy-something-year-old aunt was in a catfight. I hid in the corner of the room with my face buried in the wall while strangers broke it up.

Walking home from the ticket office, Aunty Doe was exhilarated.

Not long after my return to New York, Aunty Doe packed her bags—for the last time, as it turned out—and flew to Las Vegas to visit her son, Larry, and his current wife, Pat.

In the middle of the night, Larry and Pat were awakened by a loud thud. They rushed into the guest room where they found Aunty Doe collapsed on the floor like a rag doll. She had suffered a massive stroke. From then on, Uncle Jim spent as much time as he could in Las Vegas visiting my aunt in a fancy but none-the-less repellent nursing home.

Over the next three years, I flew out when I could to see Aunty Doe. Her suffering appalled me. She was a ghost, a wraithlike scrap of what she had been. "Take me home!" she pleaded constantly. "Take me home!" I thought the tubes keeping her alive were instruments of torture.

"Can't you bring her home?" I asked Uncle Jim. But all he could do was shrug his shoulders impotently and sigh.

Through the years, I had seen few outward signs of affection between my uncle and aunt. They had never kissed or hugged in front of me. Given the apparent formality of their relationship, I was stunned by the palpable love I now saw between them. The room was filled with it. I must have missed something all those years, but finally, I got it. Jimmy and Flo—like ham and eggs.

Jimmy & Flo, like Ham & Eggs

IT WAS A COLD, rainy Friday the thirteenth. I arrived at Campbell's Funeral Home where my mother and father had been laid out twenty years before. I was taken in to view the body of my aunt, who had been released finally from her agony. I kept staring at her face. Her hands. I thought of the myth of our relationship. I was always told, "Your aunt would go through fire for you. Cut off her arm for you."

But never me as a separate person. No separation allowed.

Within an hour, the room was filled with people. There were beefy men with broken noses, businessmen with their carefully coifed wives, bigwigs from Las Vegas, executives from the William

Morris Agency. There were friends of mine, who graciously showed up.

It was touching to see Anna, the woman who had cleaned the apartment and, over the years, become a friend to my aunt. And Raphael, the doorman from Fifty-Fifth Street, who shyly came to pay his respects.

Joe Adonis's daughter was there, as was the daughter of Bart Salvo, Uncle Jim's old partner from Prohibition days. These men had been especially close to my uncle and their daughters and I had grown up in parallel universes.

My husband and my two sons came up from Florida. Uncle Jim had flown in from Las Vegas on the red-eye and arrived late. People milled around, their conversations overlapping and creating a loud hum. It was like a cocktail party without the cocktails. Except that Aunty Doe lay dead in a box at the end of the room. Catching a glimpse of Uncle Jim chatting with people and seeming like his usual imperturbable self, I wondered how the man who could handle anything was going to handle this.

Under a heavy gray sky, we rode in black limousines to Woodlawn Cemetery in the Bronx, where Uncle Jim's parents and his sister, Lizzy, were buried in the Alo family plot. We were given red roses to place on the coffin, which struck me as symbolic of my aunt's enduring beauty. In the last few years of her conscious life, thanks to sweet, blessed forgetfulness, I had been Auntie Doe's special girl again. All the "why nots" and "could have beens" no longer mattered. She had loved me in the best, no—the only way she was able. And I had loved her.

Uncle Jim stood alone for a while, wanting to stay with my aunt—this contentious, wisecracking, wry, exasperating, stand-up woman with whom he had shared sixty-one years of his life. Finally, he pulled the woolen scarf tighter around his face, shielding himself from the biting wind, and walked down the grassy hill towards me.

Six months later, my uncle, revealing a deep layer of emotional naïveté, told me with unblinking honesty, "I never thought I'd miss her so much."

AN UNWELCOMED THOUGHT

After my aunt's death, I spent countless evenings with Uncle Jim in many of his favorite restaurants—and I got to know him as I never had before. Usually, his amiable pal, Sidney, joined us. The talk was of politics and the world, people and what makes them tick, old New York and the way it used to be.

I was late as I stepped out of a cab to meet my uncle in the spring of 1990. My mind flashed back to the Forties and Fifties of my childhood, when cabbies were mostly Jewish and philosophical. When there were no homeless. And you could stroll home on a summer's evening along the park or maybe even in the park and not fear for your life. I rushed up the street because I didn't want to keep my uncle waiting. He valued punctuality.

"We'll eat around the corner at L'Aperatif," Uncle Jim said in his gravelly voice. He carefully wrapped his woolen scarf around his neck and pulled on his gray fedora—his two leathery fingers gripping the hat exactly at the indentations on the front, as he located the perfect spot on his leonine head.

We entered the restaurant, gave our coats to the hatcheck girl, and took seats at the bar. Uncle Jim ordered his usual vodka tonic and I ordered a Campari and soda, a habit I picked up from my tea-totaling aunt.

The bartender placed a small bowl of salted nuts in front of us. "How are you tonight, Mr. Jimmy?" he asked with his soft accent and respectful manner. My uncle inquired about the man's family and hometown back in Italy and I observed, for the millionth time, Uncle Jim's courtliness, and his ability to appear interested in the people around him, great and small.

We moved to a table in the sparsely occupied dining room. Uncle Jim was in his eighties but looked very much the same as he always had.

The waiters hovered around while we ordered. Uncle Jim was precise, "Don't forget to chop the salad fine."

Now, we could begin to talk. Or rather, he would talk and I would listen. Tonight, Sidney wouldn't be joining us.

My relationship with my uncle deepened after my aunt's death. I became his favored companion. "This is my *niece*," he would say, introducing me with a twinkle in his eye. "My *real* niece. And, she's the spittin' image of her aunt."

On this night, he was in the mood to contemplate the past and comment on current conditions.

> People aren't the same today. Take Lillian Hellman. When she went before the House Un-American Activities Committee, you know what she said? She said, "I cannot and will not cut my conscience to fit today's fashions." She had a lotta of moxie. Who would do that today? Look at Richard Nixon. He refused to ask for a recount after he lost the election to Kennedy. Why? Because

he didn't think it would be good for the country. It's all changed now. People have no character anymore.

Uncle Jim dabbed at his mouth with a napkin.

Did I ever tell you the story about that bum, Sinatra? Well, this happened in 1970. The Italian-American Civil Rights League is havin' a rally on Columbus Circle and they ask Sinatra if he'd show up, you know, just to show solidarity, which he said he would. Now, when the time comes, he sends word that he can't make it because of an operation on his finger. Some bullshit like that. So now—I get a call from Henrí Giné that Sinatra wants to talk to me—very important. So I go over to Henrí's office in the Century Apartments, so he can call me there. Which he does. Well, Jesus Christ, he's shittin' in his pants. It's Jimmy this and Jimmy that and, "Jimmy, you gotta help me out. These guys wanna kill me." So I says to him, "Hey, Frank. Calm down. Now what's their beef?"

He says to me, "Jimmy, I tried to explain to these guys. But they say I better not come east of the Mississippi, or else!"

So I says to him, "Well, Jesus, Frank, this sounds like one hell of a situation. I tell you what I'm gonna do. I'll get ahold of Aniello Dellacroce and try to work somethin' out. Call me in two days."

So I get ahold of Aniello and tell him that Sinatra copped a plea to me, and he should forget the whole thing. To which he says, "Hey, Jimmy. No problem. We just wanted to shake the bastard up a little bit. Teach him a lesson, that's all."

Okay, so now—I go over to Henrí's office and Sinatra calls again.

"Jimmy," he says, "What's the outcome?"

Meanwhile, he's shittin' in his pants.

"Jesus, Frank," I says, "You got yourself in a jackpot here. They're really steamed!

I tell you what you do. Gimme another call in a couple a days. I'll see what I can do."

"Gee, thanks, Jimmy," he says. "You don't know how much I appreciate this."

I can tell he's sweatin' bullets.

So I stretch this thing out for about a week, with phone calls back and forth. Naturally, I never talk to Aniello again, because there's no problem. So finally I tell Sinatra, "Okay, Frank. Everything's straightened out. They finally listened to reason. But here's what they want. They want you to show up and sing a few songs when they have the big benefit, in a few months, at Madison Square Garden."

Well, Christ, by that time, he would have agreed to anything, you know? So he did show up for that, and they wound up raisin' $500,000. That was back in 1979. But anyhow, I got a big kick out of it."

Uncle Jim took a sip of his coffee and sat back serenely in his chair, relishing the memory of the big joke he once played on Frank Sinatra. It was the first time I had heard the story, but it wouldn't be the last. I wondered just what it was about this guy that bugged my uncle so much. Was it that he thought Sinatra pushed the little guys around? Got too big for his britches?

When it came to Sinatra, my competitive uncle just couldn't understand what all the fuss was about.

ME AND JIMMY BLUE EYES

ONE EVENING, I met Uncle Jim at his apartment and we walked around the corner to the Hilton Hotel. It was just the two of us and we took a quiet table in the dining room.

Uncle Jim had begun to avoid eating meat, usually preferring a fillet of sole, with a glass of wine to finish things off. "All things in moderation" was his belief, so dessert was always a shared affair with each of us getting our own fork.

On this occasion, my uncle was remembering the European trips he had made with my aunt in the last decades of their life together.

> Your aunt and I took a trip to Europe in 1966. While we were in Rome, we went to dinner one night with my old friend Dino De Laurentiis and his wife, Silvana Mangano. Nicest people in the world. Well, they were makin' *The Bible* at the time and Dino asked us if we'd like to go over to Cinecitta Studios and take a look. So the next day we went.
>
> Well, they're shootin' a scene and who comes over but John Huston, who was the director—big, tall, skinny guy. So now—we all go out to dinner together a few nights later and Huston asks me where my people come from and I tell him Calabria.
>
> "Oh, Calabria," he says. "Great people, the Calabrase."
>
> Well, Jesus, I was glad to hear him say that because all this time, I always heard that the Calabrase were a bunch of hardheaded shits.
>
> "Well, now, Jimmy," he says, "There's a wonderful book called *My Travels in Calabria*. I think it's out of print, but I'm going to send you a copy."
>
> So that was that. Now about six months go by and I forget all about it. Well, one day, this book arrives in the mail. *My Travels in Calabria*. Well, Jesus Christ, you coulda knocked me over with a

feather. It just shows you the kind of classy bum Huston was. I never forgot that.

Oh, yeah, he had this idea of having me be the voice of God in *The Bible*. Can you imagine that?

I thought to myself, you know, I'll be damned if that doesn't make perfect sense.

SOMETIMES, Sidney would drive in from his apartment on Long Island to take us on joy rides. One day, Uncle Jim wanted to visit the Bronx, where he had grown up. Being raised in a bubble the way I had, I never knew the first thing about the Bronx, Brooklyn, or any of the outlying areas surrounding Manhattan. So now, it was time for me to get a guided tour of my uncle's old stomping grounds.

What once had been an Italian ghetto now was a mixture of some Italians and mostly Latinos. I saw a butcher shop with crates of live chickens stacked up outside, ready to be sold and killed. There was a store that sold only pork and another that specialized in Italian delicacies such as Genoa salami, provolone cheese, and prosciutto. The neighborhood still had the gritty quality of the old days; and I tried to imagine my uncle as a boy, playing on the turn-of-the-century streets in knickers and lace-up shoes.

I had never given much thought to Uncle Jim's ethnicity, probably because in their household, my aunt's Irish background predominated. But now that she was gone, he seemed to become more Italian by the minute. At home, he preferred drinking his coffee out of a glass, and he could frequently be found digging his way with great gusto through a steaming bowl of pasta. Age and Time were reacquainting him with his roots.

One afternoon, Sidney drove us down into Little Italy. We stopped for dinner and I was surprised to find that Jimmy Blue Eyes was as known and welcomed there as he was uptown. The restaurant proprietor visited our table and his hand lingered on my uncle's shoulder as if he was picking up a special charge of wise guy energy as they chatted.

We drove through the Lower East Side, where Meyer and Ben Siegel had grown up. Uncle Jim seemed to be reliving his past, and he wanted to show me the places where his early life had played out.

I spent many hours and days eavesdropping from the back seat as Uncle Jim and Sidney talked about the good old, bad old days. They laughed about people, including themselves, wildly waving guns around. I even got the idea that my uncle might have been involved in a bank robbery or two. Sidney had—and spent eighteen years of his life in jail because of it.

The curtain was lifting just a bit…

> I met Uncle Jim and Sidney at Joe & Rose's on the East Side. As usual, first a drink at the bar—then to a table in the back opposite a mural of Capri. After we ordered, it was clear that Uncle Jim was in the mood to reminisce.
>
> Did I ever tell you about the time we heard there was this "Mustachio Pete" who was makin' a lotta money up in the Bronx?

Well, we were doin' great sellin' beer up in Westchester, when my partner, Bart, mentioned a guy up in the Bronx who was doin' three or four thousand a day.

"Who the hell is this guy?" I ask him.

"He's nobody," Bart says. "A greaseball from Italy."

I say to Bart, "Let's go see him. And let me do the talkin'."

We go up to New Rochelle and we go to see this guy at his office. So we go in and I have a forty-five in my pants and I open my jacket a little so he can see it. We introduce ourselves and I tell the guy, "Okay, you're outta business."

He jumps up outta his chair! "Whatya you mean, I'm outta business?" he says.

"As of tomorrow, you're outta business and we're takin over," I tell him. "Otherwise, you'll suffer the consequences."

And that was how we got into the numbers business. The greaseball went and complained to Charlie Lucky, but naturally, Charlie favored us.

UNCLE JIM and Sidney are laughing like hell.

"But, Uncle," I say, pretending to concentrate on buttering my bread. "Wasn't that a lousy thing to do?"

He shrugs his shoulders. "Yeah," he says, thoughtfully.

On New Year's Eve, my friend, Julie Morgan, and I walked down Third Avenue to Abe's Steak House where we met my uncle at the bar. The occasion was commemorated with photos taken in front of colorful balloons. Uncle Jim was in rare form and at his most congenial with my beautiful, blonde friend. It was hard to tell who was charming whom.

Julie had the impression that when we walked to our table, the waves parted. After we were seated, she recalls two young wise guys coming to the table to pay their respects. Her impression was that they did everything but genuflect and kiss Uncle Jim's ring.

Another friend confided to me her fear that I would be mowed down by machine guns some night while eating out with my uncle.

People see too many movies.

THERE ARE moments that come upon you when you least expect it.

One day, in the subway, as I was hurtling through the labyrinth of tunnels beneath the city, a word leapt from my subconscious and appeared as if on a movie screen in my head.

MURDERER!

The question presented itself like an unwelcome intruder. *Is Uncle Jim a murderer?* Tears flooded my eyes and I was grateful for the dark glasses that shielded me from the other passengers. All my life, I had heard the rumors that had been directed at my uncle. And dismissed them. Until that moment, it had never occurred to me that any of them was true. Could be true. But just for an instant, something lurking within my consciousness had broken through.

What really happened to the "dear friend" Ben Siegel? If Jimmy Blue Eyes was Meyer Lansky's "muscle"—what exactly did that mean? What ominous truths might be hidden beneath the cloistered surface of our lives? My uncle and aunt carried on all these years as if the circumstances of their life were somehow normal.

But didn't I know my uncle? Was I going to believe a world of people who had never even met him? Or was I going to trust my instincts and a lifetime of up-close and personal contact? I wanted to believe that I could tell a *good* person from a *bad* one.

These questions had never concerned me until now. But in that one strange moment, a veil had suddenly been lifted and the word *murderer* had appeared, unbidden, in my mind.

ACE IN THE HOLE

When I performed my cabaret show at Eighty-Eights, in the Village, Uncle Jim came every night. He was there when Rex Reed showed up with my friend, veteran Broadway star, Benay Venuta. And he was there on the night that Liza Minnelli showed up. Mercifully, *nobody told me she was there*—because if I had known, I would have gone into paralyses. As it turned out, she was warm and gracious.

I included in my show the Simon and Garfunkel Song, "The Boxer," which I dedicated to my father—and an old, turn-of-the-century song, "Ace in the Hole," I had heard Uncle Jim sing:

> *This town is full of guys who think they're mighty wise*
> *Just because they know a thing or two*
> *You'll meet them night and day Strolling up and down Broadway*
> *Telling of the wonders that they do.*
> *There's con men and there's boosters, there's card men and crap shooters*
> *They congregate around the Metropole*
> *They wear fancy ties and collars, but the way they get their dollars*

They all have got an Ace stuck in the Hole...

I meant this as an homage to my uncle, now almost ninety—who, for better or for worse, had always been my ace in the hole.

ONE NIGHT, after the show, Uncle Jim spoke about his relationship with Mike Todd.

"Mike Todd wanted me to invest in *Around the World in Eighty Days;* but like a dope, I said 'no.' He hounded me so bad, I hadda duck him. Too bad he's not around today. I could of done somethin' for you."

This remark really burned me. All my life I worked to get out of my uncle's spotlight and into my own. *On* my own. He never understood that. Maybe he enjoyed being helpful—but his kind of help weakened and diminished people in the long run. He always had to be the kingpin. If you didn't *need him*, then, *he* didn't need *you*.

Finally getting his approval and having him see me—in my own light—had been like pulling teeth. So now, Uncle Jim was back in a cabaret room again, like the old days, only this time, I was the featured attraction.

One night after a show, he told a friend of mine, "I didn't think she had it in her."

Well, Uncle Jim. I did.

IF ALL OF this had taken place twenty years earlier, the story might have been different. I was fifty-one. I had returned to New York chasing what I thought would be true success. What I found was some failure, some success and a deeper knowledge and acceptance of myself. In New York I survived the brutality of show business and the anguish of solitude.

My husband, Joe, and I had maintained a long distance relationship. Miraculously, during the time I was away we developed a new and closer bond. I had finally proved myself to myself; and I decided it was time to pack up my music, my photos, my reviews, and my memories and return to the 1924 farmhouse that had been the magnificent obsession and beloved work-in-progress of my husband and myself ever since we stumbled upon it in a state of dilapidation twenty years before. The house, like our marriage, had always had good bones and lots of potential. What was required was a little tender loving care.

As for Uncle Jim, one night, as he was turning the key at the front door of his apartment building, a man came up behind him with a gun, intending to rob him. Uncle Jim turned, punched the thief, and then chased the startled man down the street. At eighty-eight, he still had a pretty good left hook. He continued to follow his usual habit of spending time in Florida, traveling to New York every month or so and flying to Vegas to visit friends and family whenever the spirit moved him.

In Florida, he had a new sidekick by the name of Tommy who was an ex-hairdresser and wanna-be tough guy. I had met Tommy when he was doing hair on a film I'd appeared in a few years earlier. He idolized Uncle Jim and believed that just being in his presence was a major life accomplishment. He repeated many times that Uncle Jim was—*the greatest person he had ever met... had taught him so much about how to be a man.*

Tommy made himself useful to Jimmy Blue Eyes in a variety of ways. He took care of the car, babysat the house, and was available for errands of all kinds. He also provided Uncle Jim with the male companionship he required. In return, Uncle Jim helped Tommy with money from time to time and granted him the privilege of his company.

During the next few years, my uncle grew close to my youngest son, Kevin. When Kevin married a petite and beautiful Swedish girl named Isabel, Uncle Jim was there to share in our happiness.

Uncle Jim had no shortage of friends and dined with someone different every night. It became a habit for Kevin, Isabel, Joe, and me to have dinner with him at least once a week. We usually met at either Pier 5, across from Gulfstream Racetrack or Christine Lee's at the Thunderbird Hotel on Miami Beach.

My very astute son, Kevin, made sure to read the *New York Times* before each meeting. He knew discussions of current events would make up much of the conversation and he wanted to keep up. As it turned out, not only did Uncle Jim want to discuss world events—he wanted to talk about his *life*.

"When I sold my interest in the Sands, I arranged for your cousins to hold my money because I was in the can at the time. Lawrence had $600,000 and Billy had $250,000. When I got out, it was all gone. I was stupefied."

"What do you mean?" I asked him, shocked.

"They spent it. They both were gamblers, you know. Larry had the nerve to tell me that Frannie said the money was 'no good' and burned it in the kitchen sink. Well, who the hell did he think he was kiddin'? What was I gonna do? Kill them? They were your aunt's sons. I couldn't hurt her—so I forgot about it."

Joe & Carole together again

That was Uncle Jim. Able to take the loss of close to a million dollars, betrayal by members of his own family—and just blow it off. Not because the money wouldn't have come in handy. And not because he wasn't capable of banishing bad apples from his life—but because expediency was one of the major ingredients in his personality.

∼

ONE NIGHT, during dinner, Uncle Jim talked about the first time he went to jail:

> Society made me what I became. I worked on Wall Street for five years and went to night school at the same time. Till I realized I wasn't gettin' promoted like the others. At that time there were no Italians workin' on Wall Street. Well, I knew I wasn't stupid, so I said, "Screw this!" Then I went the other way. You did what you could to make some money. I got caught stickin' up a jewelry store. They gave me the maximum sentence, twelve to fifteen years. With my pedigree—a first offense and five years working on Wall Street—hell, I was a real good candidate for rehabilitation. They wanted me to tell them who the other three guys were. Well, I couldn't do that. Because, as far as I was concerned, a snitch was a snitch, whether it was in school or on the street. And I couldn't turn my pals in, who I knew all my life. So they sent me to Sing Sing. After I got there, the priest came to see me—a real son-of-a-bitch. He said, "Vincent, I'd like to have a talk with you. I think I can help you. Why don't you tell me who those other boys were?" I said to myself, "The hell with you!" If I got this far and didn't snitch on my friends, I sure as hell wasn't gonna tell anything to this priest. So I just told him the same story I told before. That I met a few fellas at the pool hall and didn't know their names. I did almost five years. And by the time I got out I was a GOOD CRIMINAL. I never had another nine-to-five job.

"When you robbed the store," Isabel asked, "how did the police identify you?"

"It wasn't difficult," he said, "since I was the one runnin' away with a bag of jewelry in my hand."

The next day, Uncle Jim called Kevin to say, "Jeez, I hope Isabel doesn't think I'm a common crook."

Kevin and Isabel were a law abiding young couple who were in line to hear some outlandish things in the next few years. It's to their credit that they were able to take it all in while applying a large dose of good humor.

ANOTHER EVENING, another restaurant. Uncle Jim was again in the mood to reminisce:

> This is back in the Thirties. Bart and Tommy and I are in the numbers business. One of our people was havin' some trouble with a runner who's working for the Dutchman [Dutch Schultz]. I'm in Hot Springs, takin the baths, and I get a call from Bart to tell me about it and I tell him not to do anything till I get there. When I arrive in New York, Bart and I go up to New Rochelle to a club or hall where these guys congregate.
>
> I ask Bart, "How big is this guy?"
>
> "About your size," he tells me.
>
> "Okay, then, don't you do anything," I say.
>
> Sure enough, the guy comes along. So I go up to him and tap him on the shoulder. "Say, I'd like to have a word with you."
>
> With that, he shoves me aside and tells me, "Get outta here!"

"Well, *Bam!* I give him a shot and down he goes. Then I hoof him a couple a' times. Boy, was I mad! Now, a few days later, I'm over at the Beresford [Hotel] where some of the boys had a runnin' card game. Ben Siegel was there, along with Moey Sedway and Bo Weinberg, who worked for the Dutchman.

Well, Bo Weinberg, who was a hell of a nice guy, starts talkin' about this runner who went back to the Dutchman and complained that he had the hell beat outta him by three or four guys.

I start laughin'. "Say, Bo," I tell him. "I was those three or four guys."

ONE NIGHT, we went to a tacky Italian restaurant on Collins Avenue that Uncle Jim liked because, "They have a good chef." As Joe, Kevin, Isabel, and I concentrated on our pasta, we began to notice a conversation going on between the barmaid and a customer at the bar.

"Oh, yeah, my father is in this book, *The Little Man*, about Meyer Lansky."

Uncle Jim's ears perked up.

The barmaid continued, "My father was one of Meyer Lansky's best friends."

Uncle Jim spoke to the girl. "What's that, your father knew Meyer Lansky?"

"Yeah," she answered. "Why? Did you know Meyer?"

"Yeah."

"Well, what's your name?" she asks.

"Well, I won't tell you my *nickname*, but my *name* is Jimmy Alo."

"My father bought a hotel from Meyer with the stipulation that Meyer's retarded son could work there."

"He wasn't retarded," said Uncle Jim. "He was crippled."

At this point, a waiter quietly informed the barmaid that the person she was talking to was Jimmy Blue Eyes. With that, she became very excited and rushed to the phone to call her father. She quickly returned and asked Uncle Jim to please come to the phone and speak to her father—which Uncle Jim reluctantly did. When he returned to the table, he was grinning from ear to ear. "Ha, ha. I probably made his day."

Uncle Jim got a big kick out of being who he was.

CHEWING GUM AND PLATINUM HAIR

Although he hated to do it, Uncle Jim decided to sell the house that he and my aunt had built together in Florida. It had been a monument to all he had accomplished and a commentary on the mediocrity from which he had escaped. He held onto it for a long time after Aunty Doe was gone. Still, it must have seemed like a hollow space filled with a million memories.

An architect and his wife, an interior designer, made an offer on the house. Not long after the deal was set, I met Hope, the new owner.

"Your uncle is fantastic," she told me. "When he came to the door he was wearing the most gorgeous trousers and sweater. And I noticed his shoes! Everything about him was just amazing. I went home and told my mother about him. I only wish I could have met him ten years ago—and had a chance to be around him."

"Do you know anything about him?" I asked, delicately.

"No," she said, feigning innocence. "Nothing."

Hard to believe that she didn't know *exactly* who he was before she ever knocked on the door.

UNCLE JIM and I went apartment hunting. He was looking for something in one of the high rises on Hallandale Beach. The glamour and exclusivity of my uncle's day had given way to sprawling commercialism—shopping malls crawling with people and high rises popping up incessantly, creating bland, concrete chasms. "Who's gonna live in all these joints?" Uncle Jim asked, shaking his head.

In due course, he settled on the Sea Air Towers on Ocean Drive. When we went there to have a look, we visited the coffee shop. As we entered, a man with his nose somewhat on the side of his face approached us. He greeted us warmly, explaining that he was the proprietor.

"Do I know you?" my uncle asked.

"I'm from Brooklyn, Jimmy. I know you. You probably don't remember me." The man spoke with an accent that confirmed his place of origin. He treated Jimmy Blue Eyes with the respect usually reserved for royalty. At that moment, Uncle Jim felt at home. This man knew him. It was a connection. I was relieved because I realized what a misery it was for him to let go of the house and move somewhere else. When we went for our car, the guy who ran the parking concession made it clear that *he* knew who Uncle Jim was. The word had already gotten around.

Now I had the task of disposing of the overwhelming amount of "stuff" the house contained.

With the help of my friend, Geri, I made decisions as to what I wanted to keep.

I brought home the linens, which were moldy and mildewed—and the three sets of china from the kitchen cabinets. As I worked on the old tablecloths and napkins, draping them across garden chairs so that the sun could bleach them white again, I suddenly felt Hattie so close to me. I could picture her handling these objects—sitting at the mangler in the cool of the garage or hanging them on the line to dry beside the orange tree at the back of the kitchen. It was Hattie who had supplied the hugs and kisses that I can't recall receiving from anyone else in my childhood.

It was as if these inanimate things had a living quality to them. They had fallen into neglect and disrepair; and by restoring them, it seemed that I was in some way displaying a tenderness and caring that I had never been able to extend to my aunt.

It was my job to furnish Uncle Jim's apartment with things from Monroe Street. And though he claimed that none of it mattered, it made me feel better to see to it that familiar things surrounded him.

Soon the place looked like him: cool and serene, with pale blue walls, his half-moon walnut desk in front of the large window that overlooked the blue Atlantic.

After working like crazy for months on every aspect of moving my uncle from his house to the new apartment—I called him on the morning of the move, telling him, "I'm on my way."

"Don't rush," he says.

"What do you mean?" I asked him.

"I don't want you to go out of your way."

I'll never forget the sight of my uncle, sitting on the low concrete wall that surrounded the house, his chin resting on his hands. As the movers carried things, piece by piece into the massive van, he looked like a lost little boy. I could tell from the droop of his head and the dejected shape of his body that he was hurting. I had never seen him this way. Later, when he talked about that day, he said, "I felt like I was losin' my best friend."

It felt surreal as I led the movers to my uncle's new residence across the lake. I showed them the way to the beachside high rise where I had attempted to create a miniature version of the home he was leaving behind.

"Uncle Jim," I said at the end of the day. "That's some fabulous view you've got there."

"It's the ocean," he answered glumly. "I've seen it."

The only thing that cheered him up was the knowledge that if you stood at the far end of his small balcony and looked to the west, across the Intercoastal Waterway, you could actually see the house on Monroe Street.

He had everything he needed to make him comfortable. I had decorated the living room walls with photographic portraits of my aunt taken in the Forties and lots of black-framed photos of Uncle Jim with celebrities and friends, smiling his million-dollar smile. Everywhere, were trinkets, tokens, and mementos of the past. In his nineties—the past was all Uncle Jim was thinking about.

After a week or two, he settled in. He greased a few palms here, told a few stories there, grumbled, and complained—and made himself at home.

I COULD SEE the ways in which Tommy was important to Uncle Jim. More than anything else, Tommy helped my uncle maintain his sense of himself as he had always been. The macho man. The Chief.

Tommy was dying to get a book written about Uncle Jim. He located a writer who was supposed to come up with a treatment. A meeting was arranged between the writer and me at a New York restaurant on the Upper East Side. After the young man and I talked for twenty minutes or so, he looked at me quizzically and said, "You're not exactly what I had expected."

"What *did* you expect?" I asked him. "Chewing gum and platinum hair?"

The writer was friendly with the daughter of Dustin Hoffman. Hoffman was getting ready to portray Dutch Schultz in a movie called *Billy Bathgate*, and he had expressed an interest in meeting with Uncle Jim, who had actually *known* the Dutchman. Several meetings were arranged, and canceled. Finally, the writer told me that Hoffman was "too busy," and had commented that he didn't really *need* to meet Jimmy Blue Eyes because, after all, "it's only a movie."

After the third cancellation, Uncle Jim shrugged. He took it all with an air of nonchalance. Personally, I think Dustin Hoffman missed a golden opportunity to observe the real deal. Watching actors, even the most gifted ones, attempting to play mobsters is usually laughable. Aside from a few notable exceptions, they overdo.

I never heard anything more from Tommy about the so-called book.

∽

THE FAMILY WAS HAVING dinner with Uncle Jim at Pier 5. He tapped his knife on the glass to get the waiter's attention.

"Say, tell those loud people at the next table to come up for air, will ya?"

Later, he applauded when they left. This was not Uncle Jim's usual behavior, but rather, it was a ninety-year-old exercising his entitlement. To distract him, I initiated a story.

"Uncle Jim, I don't think you've ever told us about your first date with Aunty Doe."

"Oh. Well, we went for Chinese food on Columbus Circle. Then we took a walk afterwards. This is funny. We were talking about this and that. People we knew. And your aunt says, 'Now don't introduce me to that Jimmy Blue Eyes.' And I says, 'Why?' 'Because,' she says, "I hear he's a terrible person.'"

Uncle Jim laughed.

"Was she shocked when she found out who you were?"

"No, because by that time she already knew I was a nice guy."

Uncle Jim began to give a lot of thought to the ways he had been "screwed" in his life. It was as if, up until this point, he had known these things but didn't think it was worth bothering about. Now so many loved ones were gone. Youth was gone. With life becoming less rewarding than it had once been, there was time to reflect on the injustices and the betrayals.

He began to ruminate over Aunty Doe's friend, Lilyan Lewis. She and her husband, Moe, had been part of my uncle and aunt's close circle of friends throughout the Seventies and Eighties. Lilyan had traveled to Europe with them and joined them aboard the yacht that took them on their fondly-remembered Mediterranean cruise.

Uncle Jim had been instrumental in landing Moe the position of Entertainment Manager at the Sands Hotel in Las Vegas. Later, after the "boys" were gone from the Sands, Moe was booking performers into the Stardust Hotel and getting kickbacks from small acts. A group from Chicago took over the Stardust and wanted to fire Moe, who was suffering with cancer at the time. He had an insurance policy that paid out forty thousand dollars if he died at home or in the hospital, but eighty thousand if he died on the job. Uncle Jim appealed to the Chicago people to keep him on, telling them it was, "no skin off their noses." They did, and when Moe died Lilyan received the eighty thousand. "Not a bad score," said Uncle Jim.

When Aunty Doe passed away, the reception after the funeral was held at Lilyan's New York apartment. It wasn't until almost a decade had passed that Uncle Jim began to reflect on the fact that, during my aunt's entire illness in Las Vegas, Lilyan had never once visited her.

"All your aunt kept sayin' was, 'Lilyan. Where is Lilyan?'" Everybody who walked into the Goddamned room was *Lilyan*. So where the hell was she?"

He stopped speaking to Lilyan, and she couldn't understand why. She tried to explain that Moe had been dying of cancer, and she couldn't take any more sickness during that dark time. Uncle Jim would hear none of it.

"I changed their whole life!" he said with anguish. "I been around a long time. The beauty part of livin'... how can I word it? Havin' friends."

The betrayals weighed heavily on him now. "It's the story of my life. Lilyan, Malnik. Lois Wood. Jesus Christ tried to straighten out human nature. Even He couldn't do it."

Tommy and Uncle Jim were always trying to come up with ways to get some satisfaction, some compensation out of Al Malnik. Because it was he who had caused Uncle Jim to go to jail. They came up with various schemes for wringing some money or favor out of him, but nothing ever panned out.

One night, Uncle Jim was enjoying himself at a party when a friend approached him and said, "Jimmy, there's somebody here who would like to say 'hello' to you. It's Lois Pope. Can I bring her over?"

Surprised, but feeling magnanimous, Uncle Jim gave the okay. Moments later, the former Lois O'Brien Wood, was gushing with explanations about her treatment of him and of my aunt. Thirty years earlier, she had jettisoned their friendship, after her engagement to Generoso Pope. Now, she wanted to be exonerated. She invited Uncle Jim to come to dinner at her home on the ocean in Manalapan, just south of Palm Beach. "Okay," said Uncle Jim. "I'll come up with Carole." Why did he accept the invitation? I doubt that he was curious. Most likely, he thought in his narcissistic way, "What the hell. I'll give her a break."

Lois had come a long way since the days when she was singing for her supper. When Generoso Pope died, the *National Enquirer*, along with its sister publications, were sold for $412 million. Lois became a philanthropist. In 1996, she donated ten million to the University of Miami for medical research.

I made arrangements through her social secretary and, on the designated day, Joe and I drove to Lois's house together with Uncle Jim, Kevin, and Isabel. We passed through massive gates to a mansion that looked more like a bank than a home. Inside, I was immediately convinced that this was *not* Lois's home, but a movie set staged for a remake of *The Fountainhead*.

There was not one personal object in sight. It seemed like a showroom. Lois herself had not changed much over the years. She was still slim, still wore the same blonde chignon, though there was no longer a flower in her hair. It felt strange to be with her again, as if differing time zones had collided; but I detected no acknowledgement of our past friendship.

The big surprise was that Al Malnik was joining us for dinner. It turned out that he and Lois were pals. After a drink in the massive living room, we were led into a small, round dining room where we were seated according to name cards on the table.

Servers padded in to deliver each course of the catered meal. The atmosphere was awkward and bizarre and I thought it was a mistake to have come.

Lois and Malnik were seated next to each other and kept up a steady stream of conversation in which they sounded like a couple of politicians who knew the cameras were on them.

"Lois, I just can't tell you how impressed I am with the tremendous contributions you've made to society."

"Oh, Al, please don't embarrass me. And you know, I could certainly say the same to you in light of all the wonderful things you've done in your life."

Such great humanitarians! They just couldn't congratulate each other enough. In Lois's case, at least there is documentation of her public generosity. As for Malnik, I'm not sure as to why he appeared so pleased with himself. Since the conversation had nothing to do with Uncle Jim, he quietly concentrated on his dinner.

Why had my uncle agreed to break bread with Lois? He should have shunned her, the way she once shunned him and my aunt, who were godparents to her daughter, Michelle, for God's sake! She didn't deserve to be forgiven for dumping these two people who had been so kind to her. I couldn't help wondering what my uncle was thinking and why the hell we were there.

On the long ride home, Uncle Jim, who had been uncharacteristically silent throughout the evening, finally spoke.

> I guess a lotta people took advantage of me because I trusted them. Take Malnik. He's as phony as a three-dollar bill. I gave him $50,000 to invest in something for me right before I went to the can. When I came out three years later, he gave me my money back—and not a penny more. He said he "couldn't do business with me." And this is the bastard who caused me to go to jail! I never knew about people like him. Or Lois Wood. I was used to people I had known all my life. Like Meyer and Charlie. You could trust them with your life. So I thought everybody would be like that. I got a lotta disappointments.

THE GOLDEN YEARS

As we approached the end of the century, age began to take its toll on Uncle Jim. He still maintained his schedule of monthly visits to New York (I had the idea that he still collected revenue from the old numbers business in the Bronx)—and Las Vegas several times a year to see the family out there. But the lean frame, which hadn't changed over the years, was becoming frail.

He scoffed at the idea of a cane, so I held his arm when we walked into a restaurant or visited his bank. Joy, the Bank Lady, showered him with attention when he wanted information about his account or needed to withdraw money. He'd always ask the same question. "What's my bottom line?"

He wasn't in the habit of reading bank statements and he never owned a credit card. He was accustomed to dealing in good old, un-traceable cash.

Spending so much time with him, I was struck by the poignancy of old age. Sometimes, he was angry.

"The Golden Years," he would mutter, "Who're they kiddin'?"

One afternoon, as I drove him along busy Hallandale Boulevard, he gazed quietly out the window at what he had once considered his domain.

"Was I a good guy or a bad guy?" He said softly. "I'm an enigma, even to myself. His words took my breath away. He was adding up the score.

It was 1998 and Uncle Jim was ninety-four. I flew to New York with him. He'd finally conceded that it was unwise to travel alone. He hated having to use a wheelchair at the airport. In his mind, he was still the same old virile Jimmy.

Uncle Jim's nephew, Frankie Jr., picked us up at La Guardia Airport and drove us into Manhattan. Unlike my uncle's youngest brother, Joe, the plastic surgeon, Frankie Sr., had remained a neighborhood guy who made his living as a bookmaker.

I never met Frankie Jr., or even knew he existed until after my aunt's death. It was then that Uncle Jim began bringing me out to Frankie's house on Long Island. Frankie was the only nephew, a blood relative, and for my uncle, an important family tie.

We arrived at Uncle Jim's apartment and the three of us sat in the living room.

"Uncle Jim," I began. "I don't think it's a good idea for you to stay here by yourself anymore."

"Well, Carole, it wouldn't be proper for you to stay with me because someone might get the wrong impression." Good old Uncle Jim, still thinking someone might see him as a stud and not realize that I was his niece. "His *real* niece," as he liked to assure people.

"I'm not suggesting I stay here, Uncle Jim. I think you should go out and stay at Frankie's. He has a big house and you'll be comfortable there."

I didn't win the argument, but it was clear that the time for Uncle Jim to be making his way around the city on his own was coming to a close.

SOON WE WERE BACK in Florida. One of Uncle Jim's favorite hangouts was a diner across from Gulf Stream Race Track, called Flashback. It was as close to a New York Deli as you could get. Photos of Clark Gable, James Dean, Marilyn Monroe, and other vintage movie stars gazed down blankly from the walls like so many trophies.

The place was a popular hangout for a wide range of people and we went there often for lunch. Part of its appeal for Uncle Jim was the owner, an ageless Greek woman named Elizabeth. She had a charming accent and joie de vivre—and she flirted with him shamelessly, which he loved. His body may have been shrinking, but his giant male ego was firmly intact.

Proudly walking without the aid of a cane, Uncle Jim would move slowly down the aisle to a booth at the far end. The waitresses all knew him.

"Is Elizabeth here?" he would ask.

"She's in the back, Jimmy."

"Well, tell her to come out. And close those blinds. It's too bright in here."

Before long, Elizabeth would slide into the red Naugahyde seat next to him.

"Jeemy! How you doing?" she would gush.

"Well, Elizabeth . . ." He'd pause thoughtfully. "I've been thinking. How would you like it if you and I took a trip to New York?"

"Oh, you know, Jeemy, that would be great! When we going?"

"I'll have to check my schedule and get back to you," he'd say—breaking into a big Cheshire Cat grin. Elizabeth would laugh and hug him. For Uncle Jim, that was better medicine than could ever be dispensed in any doctor's office.

One afternoon, after an Elizabeth encounter, the outgoing couple in the next booth struck up a conversation with Uncle Jim. They were charmed by him. As they left, they shook our hands warmly and wished us well. When they were gone, Uncle Jim looked at me and shrugged.

"They don't know I'm the terrible Jimmy Blue Eyes," he said, wistfully.

My uncle seems to be transforming before my eyes. He comes up with a bright red jacket to go with his red and gold Miami Hurricanes canvas hat. He resurrects a pair of forty-year-old shoes. Very sporty. Navy and beige, like golfing shoes. They attract a lot of attention.

Everywhere he goes, people look at him and murmur, "Isn't he cute?"

"Cute."

"So cute."

He's turned into an elf-like being. Leaving his cane behind, he forges forward on his bowed legs, even managing to swagger a bit. It's all done with will power.

He's happy with himself. In restaurants, he smiles at everyone, hesitating for a moment as if waiting to be recognized. There's a sweetness in it.

"I've become a celebrity in my old age," he says.

I clean his eyeglasses and, if necessary, cut his meat. But he still pulls out a roll of bills at the end of the meal and takes care of the check. He tips whoever seats us and remembers to slip the busboy a dollar. He's one of a dying breed.

We were at a little Italian joint located in a motel on Miami Beach, where Joe DiMaggio ate every night. DiMaggio spotted Uncle Jim seated beneath the masses of plastic grapes hanging from the ceiling, and came over to say hello. I was shocked at how old and haggard the legendary ballplayer looked.

After he left, Uncle Jim started talking about Marilyn Monroe. How she had been treated by the Kennedy brothers, and how much DiMaggio despised them. Uncle Jim couldn't agree more.

> On the day of the assassination, I was at the barbershop in the afternoon. The shoeshine boy asked me if I'd heard the news. I asked him, "What news is that?"
>
> "The president was shot in Dallas."
>
> "Good," I said.
>
> A few years later, they killed that other dirty bastard, Bobby.
>
> If the old man didn't wanna make his son President, he would'na wound up havin' two sons assassinated. I would'na gone to jail.

Hoffa would'na gone to jail and then got killed. All this because of the machinations of Joe Kennedy. A dirtier son-of-a-bitch never lived. And he really paid for it. He ruined his whole family.

I'll tell you a story. The summer before the presidential election, an old friend of mine, Eddie McGrath, calls and says that Phil Regan wants to see me. He has a message from the Kennedys. Phil was a mutual friend, an ex-actor—and he was in the Kennedy circle. We met for lunch at the Seaview on Collins Avenue. Phil says the Kennedy people need to win in Chicago and could I do anything?

"You mean they want help from me? Are you sure?"

"Sure, I'm sure," Phil says.

"Naw, I never get involved in politics," I tell him. It was the worst mistake I ever made. I should've said "yes," and then done nothin'. But I told the truth. So they went to Sinatra, who was pallin' around with Sam Giancana at the time. Giancana threw his weight around and pulled in Cooks County for them. Let me tell you, a lotta dead people voted for Kennedy in Chicago. Kennedy won by the smallest margin ever. After the election, he showed his appreciation by dropping Sinatra like a hot potato. At the time, Morganthau was the Attorney General for New York. The word came down from Bobby Kennedy to "get something on Alo." Bobby was a vindictive son-of-a-bitch. Later, I was called to testify before the SEC about Scopitone, and they cooked me up.

A FEW DAYS later I was at a restaurant in Hollywood having lunch with Uncle Jim. I was still thinking about the Kennedys— and what he had told me several days before.

"Uncle," I asked, "What do you think about people who say that the mob was involved with the assassination of President Kennedy?"

He went on at length:

> "What would the underworld have gained? They never would have used a guy like Oswald. Wouldn't the government have nailed them immediately if there was really a connection? Instead, they buried the info until the year 2010, when nobody's gonna be alive. Who are they kidden'? Use logic. It doesn't make sense. I think the CIA did it. Because they were afraid he would give away the store, since he was romancing that broad from East Germany. East Germany was communist at the time. I think they were afraid of what Kennedy might let slip. They went to an ex-FBI agent named Mayhew, who worked for Howard Hughes in Vegas. He made the connection with Johnny Rosselli, who was with Giancana in Chicago. They gave Giancana the contract on Castro. He thought by killin' Castro, they'd be doin' a great thing. He never should've taken it. Never should've gotten involved with politics. I knew Giancana well. I thought he was a nut. He was the one who helped put Kennedy over the top in the presidential election. Then he went around braggin' about it. That's why Bobby Kennedy had a list of people he wanted to get even with after his brother was elected. Jimmy Hoffa was on the list. They framed him and sent him to jail. I was on the list because I wouldn't help them when they asked. Those sons-of-bitches were no damned good. As soon as they got in, they started goin after people."

"But, why would they go after people who helped get them elected?"

"Because they wanted to come out clean as the driven snow. They wanted to squelch any rumors linkin' them to those kind of people. Eventually, they even dumped Sinatra. Kennedy and Sinatra were no damned good. Everybody knew what was goin' on out at the Cal-Neva Lodge and Sinatra's house in Hot Springs. He built a new section onto his house because he thought it was gonna be the Western White House. But when Kennedy got elected, he snubbed Sinatra and went out there and stayed with Bing Crosby. That's the kind of rat he was.

"What right did Kennedy have to make his brother Attorney General? A guy who had never even tried a case, for Christ sake! He got criticized for it, but what did he care? He was in power and nobody could do anything about it. The old man was the cause of everything. He wanted a son to be President. Because of his ambition, his two sons were assassinated.

"And I went to the can!

"John Kennedy, Bobby Kennedy, and Martin Luther King were all killed for the same reason. They were all populists. The special interests in this country don't like populists. Remember what Eisenhower said. 'Beware the military/industrial complex.' And they're in charge of the CIA. I don't know how they did it, but that's what I think happened."

UNCLE JIM HAD REACHED the age where he was reliving and re-evaluating his life. He had a collection of stories that we would hear over and over again. He would usually begin with, "Say, did I ever tell you about the time . . . ?" and we would dutifully listen. Truth be told, it was not that much of a chore. He was endlessly interesting. If you dared to interrupt or change the subject or get up to go to the bathroom, he would say, "Wait a minute, I'm not finished."

One of his all-time favorites was the Cox story.

"Did I ever tell you about the time I wanted to go to Eglin Air Force Base?"

Joe Kevin, Isabel, and I shake our heads, "no," even though we've heard it many times before.

"I was in the joint for almost three years and Christmas was comin', so I figure I should be able to do the rest of my time at Eglin, which is a low security facility and it would be more convenient for your aunt. So I go in to see the guy in charge of my case. I'll never forget, his name was Cox.

"'Cox,' I says, 'I'd like to be transferred to Eglin for the remainder of my time.'

"So he's sittin' behind his desk and he looks at me in shock. I can see my folder on his desk and in big letters it says OC.

'Oh, you can't go to Eglin, Alo,' he says, like I just asked to go to the moon.

'Why not?' I says, playin' Dickie the Dunce.

'Well,' he says, 'because you're OC.'

'OC. What's OC?' I says, like I don't know.

'Well, Alo, OC is Organized Crime. That's why you can't go to Egland.'

'Listen, Cox,' I says to him, 'I ain't got nothin' to do with those politicians in Washington!'

"Well, I'll tell you, he was speechless. So I called your aunt and told her to get ahold of a congressman I knew in Washington—this guy would steal a red-hot stove—and have him arrange for me to go to Eglin. In the meantime, I was very comfortable in Atlanta. I was working in the library, playing paddleball, studying Spanish. I had very good relations with the other men and they would come to me to settle disputes or for advice. I was havin' fun."

"I was due out on Jan 6th, but I found out that if I could dig up eight days that they owed me, I could be home for Christmas. A friend of mine in the records office said, 'Were you held without bail after sentencing?' 'Yeah. I was held over the weekend,' I lied. 'Did you report to the marshal while out on bail?' 'Yeah, I reported once a week for six weeks.' 'That's it—that gives you your extra days.'

"With that, I get a call from Cox. So I go over to his office. 'Alo,' he says, 'You're on the next bus to Eglin.'

"Well, now I don't wanna go to Eglin because I'm afraid it might screw up my gettin' home for Christmas. So I say to him, 'I don't wanna go to Eglin.' And he's shocked. 'Why not?' he asks me. 'I changed my mind,' I tell him.

"As I'm leavin', I turn to him and say, 'Oh, by the way, Cox—whatever happened to Organized Crime?'"

WHAT UNCLE JIM wanted to do was talk. He talked about his life. He talked about who had done him wrong. He talked about good friends. One day, I was complaining to him about a friend of mine who owed me money. Here's what he had to say about friendship and money:

> A friend came to see me. His name was Jerry Zarowitz. He told me he needed to make a certain connection. I was able to help him out and he got hooked up with Caesar's Palace, which was a big, new place in Vegas. So he says to me, "Jimmy you really ought to take a

piece of the place." But I wasn't interested. I told him, "No, I'm out of the business." I had gotten my money from the Sands, and I really wasn't interested in Caesar's Palace.

Well, anyway, on one of my trips to Vegas, Jerry Zarowitz comes to see me and he gives me a package. I didn't know what it was. It was about the size of a shoebox. He says to me, "Jimmy, this is for you, because you helped me out."

So I get on a plane and go back to New York and I never look in the box. Well, that night I meet a couple of friends for dinner at Bravo Johnny's. And I still have this box with me. So I open it up and there's $50,000 in the package. So like I say, sometimes you just can't help but make money.

SOME OF THE things Uncle Jim said were touching in a funny way. There were whole areas of life for which he had no interest or feelings. Like pets.

It was Thanksgiving and I had cooked the traditional meal. After dinner Kevin, Isabel, Joe, and I lingered at the table as Uncle Jim sipped his coffee. I happened to mention that my cat, Baby Blue, had been killing doves in the garden.

"Oh," asked Uncle Jim, "is she allowed to?"

That started him reminiscing about Duke, the brown Doberman Pinscher who had lived at Monroe Street during my childhood. Duke was never allowed in the house and basically thought of my grandfather as his owner and best friend. I don't recall ever seeing Uncle Jim so much as pet the dog. Eventually, Duke developed cancer.

"When Duke got cancer, he went to the animal hospital. He was there for a couple of weeks and they called me up and said he wasn't gonna make it. So I went over there to say goodbye to him. I went out to the kennel and when Duke saw me, he dragged himself over and looked up--right into my eyes. I felt funny. Somethin' happened to me. I didn't know what it was. Jesus! I had a feelin'!"

When we heard that, we didn't know whether to laugh or cry.

BLOOD OF MY BLOOD

Writers wanting to tell his story often approached Uncle Jim. Peter Maas, author of *The Valachi Papers* and *Serpico*, phoned him regularly.

Peter Maas called me up. He writes for Vanity Fair. He wanted to know if there was any truth to the rumor that Meyer had a photo of J. Edgar Hoover in a compromising position with a man—and if Hoover gave Meyer a pass because of it. Well, now, if I wanted to be a real bastard, I could've said, "Sure, I know about it." But I just couldn't do that. Because it wasn't true. It was bullshit, and I told him so.

I don't think Hoover was a homosexual. The only thing he was interested in was communism. And it wasn't true that he laid off Meyer and me. His guys were following us from the late Fifties on. I have plenty of reasons to hate the FBI. And if I had lied Maas would have had to believe me. But I couldn't do it. So I told him, "No, Meyer didn't have any such picture." I couldn't lie about it. It wouldn't be honorable.

I told him, "Listen, Peter, I didn't like the things you said about me in the Valachi book." So he says, "Let me write your book. I'll have you coming out smelling like a rose."

I said to him, "Hey. You ain't talkin' to no Valachi!"

Nicholas Pileggi, another aficionado of the underworld, was also interested in my uncle's story. Pileggi wrote *Wiseguy: Life in a Mafia Family*, which was adapted into the blockbuster movie, *Goodfellas*—and was married to the late author and filmmaker, Nora Ephron.

Uncle Jim told Pileggi, "You oughta write about Lois Pope and her ten million dollar gift to the University of Miami. Now that's a real Cinderella story."

Pileggi's response was, "I like to write about gangsters."

I said to my uncle, one day, "Uncle Jim, all those writers want to tell your story—Maas, Pileggi—wouldn't you like to tell it? It's part of history."

"No," he said. "If I did, I would have to tell it all. And I won't do that. Because nothin' we did was legal."

ALTHOUGH HE REFUSED to talk to these authors, he began to talk to me. One of the things he explained to me was the situation Italian immigrants found themselves in when they arrived in America at the beginning of the century:

> When the Italians came over here on the boats—if they had a pimple on their nose they got sent back. There was terrible discrimination against Italians in those days. People don't realize

that. If you read the book, *Blood of My Blood,* by Richard Gambino, you'll see that there was an ad for laborers in a New York paper that said:

COMMON LABOR, WHITE—1.30/1.50

COMMON LABOR, COLORED—1.25/1.40

COMMON LABOR, ITALIAN—1.15/1.25

Oh, yeah. If you walked out of your neighborhood, the Irish kids would beat the hell out of you. They called us "guineas" and "greaseballs." We were low man on the totem pole.

Joe, Kevin, Isabel, and I were having dinner with him at Pier Five when he remembered Hallandale as it once was.

"You know, when we first got here in 1935, there were fifteen-hundred people living in Hallandale. Today, there's more than that in my apartment building. Everybody in town was busted in those days. I went to see the sheriff, Walter Clark. He was a good old boy, sittin' with his feet up on the desk and his fingers in his suspenders. A real nice guy. He'd steal a red-hot stove. Those politicians—you could buy them with a ham sandwich. If we corrupted them, then they must have wanted to be corrupted. We were lucky. It was the Depression and nobody had any money but us. We spread it around—and it made us very popular."

He took a piece of bread and dunked it into his wine.

"We made this place a resort, he says. So it was illegal. So what?"

He went on to talk about an old friend who was arrested for bank robbery in 1928.

"I was on the lam when I met your aunt. The reason is that a friend of mine, Johnny McCabe, was in jail and I tried to bust him out. I must have been crazy to try it. But he was a good friend—a very sweet guy. And I know he would have done it for me. In those days, if you were a four-time loser, you faced life. He couldn't handle it. He killed himself and took two guards with him.

"So now you know about that."

On the way home, Kevin asked me if I thought Uncle Jim had ever . . . well . . . killed anybody. I answered, "I honestly don't know. What I do know is that, early in his life, he did *something* that gave people the lasting impression that they shouldn't mess with him."

UNCLE JIM SHARED an abundance of memories about the early days with Meyer and Lucky Luciano.

"There were a lotta rough guys around in those days. Those greaseballs were hard to get along with. They would want a war every week. The custom was, they'd invite you to dinner—and 'Goodbye Charlie!' That's why 'The Commission' was there. Charlie Lucky wouldn't stand for that kinda business. Everybody had to walk the straight and narrow. If something had to be done...there hadda be a good reason. It couldn't be because you didn't like the way a guy wore his hat. Charlie was a terrific guy. Always smilin'. Everybody loved him. When he got convicted, people were sick. Everybody knew there was no way he had anything to do with all that crap. They brought in prostitutes and pimps to testify against him. They cooked him up. No drugs. We despised that. We wouldn't tolerate it. And that's the way we went along. We knew what it was at an early stage and we never bothered with it. Never."

"Did you know Frank Costello?" I asked Uncle Jim.

"Frank Costello was a real nice guy. He never should've gotten involved with Vito [Genovese]. That ruined him. New York and Chicago agreed to take the Fifth at the Kefauver Hearings. But Frank thought he could outsmart them. Well, that's the kinda guy he was. He overestimated himself and they made him look like a fool. We all agreed to take the Fifth. But he did it his way. I ducked the subpoena. I went over to Naples."

"Italy?"

"No. Florida."

"What about Capone?"

"I never knew Capone, but it looks like he was a nut. He killed seven people at one time. What did he think they were, cockroaches?"

I asked Uncle Jim, "Was Charlie Lucky really the Boss of Bosses?"

"No."

"But they say he was the genius who organized all the different crime families in New York."

"No. It was Meyer. Meyer and Charlie were very close. A lot of the guys around at that time needed to be gotten under control. We wanted to make money—not kill people!"

"You mean like the St. Valentine's Day thing?"

"Well, that was ridiculous. Nobody in New York would've done a thing like that. There were a lotta crazy people around in those days. I'll show you what I mean. Dutch Schultz. He was gonna murder Dewey. Well, he hadda be stopped. Because he was crazy.

"Meyer was partners with Ben [Siegel] and Charlie and Joe A. [Adonis] in the bootlegging business. Me and my partners worked for ourselves in the beer and numbers. I was always very friendly with Meyer. We were drawn to each other, but we weren't partners at that time. The Bugs/Meyer Gang. People thought it was one person! Meyer always kept a low profile and avoided notoriety. He was a very smart guy—but not the 'genius' they make him out to be. He knew how to predict things. Figure things out. If you do this—this will happen. That put him ahead of the average guy, who doesn't think like that. He was a genius compared to most of the guys that were around. Most of those guys couldn't spell c-a-t.

"Meyer was the architect. He set up a 'Commission.' He got together with Charley Lucky, and they organized everybody. They eliminated the troublemakers. For ultimate peace. Meyer could have run the United States. In fact, that's what this country needs, to get straightened out. The Mafia."

ONE DAY, while having an early dinner with my uncle at Conca D'oro, in Hollywood, he started talking about his friend, Johnny Dunn, who was convicted in 1949 of a waterfront murder and executed. Though so many years had passed, Uncle Jim was clearly still troubled by this.

"I found out about the government a long time ago. You knew Johnny Dunn, didn't you?"

"No, Uncle, I don't think so."

"Well, they were lookin' to pin a bum rap on him and he ran away to Florida."

"Why didn't he go to Mexico, or something?"

"Didn't have to. Communication wasn't so good in those days.

"Johnny was a good friend a mine. Most of my friends were Irish or Jewish, you know. Johnny was a real nice kid. Everybody liked him. Well, I must of liked him pretty well, because he and his wife were stayin' with us down here for a few weeks. So some guy was shot up on the waterfront in New York. It was always very rough over there. The guy didn't die. He was in the hospital. Now, there was a detective up there who didn't like Johnny for some reason. Well, he was a pretty wild kid. Anyway, the guy kept denyin' that Johnny shot him and after two weeks, he died. But this detective wanted to pin it on Johnny and he finally broke him down. We told Johnny, 'Don't go up there now'. But he wanted to go up and see his family. So he was arrested and he went to the electric chair. *And he didn't do it!* I know he didn't do it, because he was down here with us, at the time. He went to the electric chair!

"Well, that's just a little bit of my history. Always remember—friendship is everything. I had some wonderful friends in my life. I would say that's the most important thing."

DOWN BUT NOT OUT

In July of 2000 I flew from New York back to Florida with Uncle Jim. A week earlier we had traveled north together. We both went out to Long Island— he to his nephew's house and I to the home of my friends, Loria Parker and her husband, Gerry Janssen. While I had spent the next few days puttering in their garden, I spoke to Frankie Jr.'s wife, Joy, daily and she mentioned that Uncle Jim was "a little under the weather." This worried me.

On the Fourth of July, although we hadn't been invited, Loria and I decided to ride out to Huntington and visit Uncle Jim. I could see right away that he was not in good shape. The house was loaded with Alo children and grandchildren who were circulating around, oblivious to the old man lying on the couch in the sunroom like a pile of wrinkled laundry.

At one point, much to her disgust, a grubby baby was shoved into Loria's reluctant arms, slathering her blouse with pureed fruit. When she went to the kitchen sink to repair the damage, Joy Alo dropped a bomb by casually commenting that it was her understanding that I *hardly ever saw my uncle* in Florida. This was a strange thing to say to my friend, particularly since it was the furthest thing from the truth.

When I sat with him, Uncle Jim seemed fuzzy and I left concerned about his condition. I was glad that we were scheduled to fly home in a few days.

When Frankie delivered Uncle Jim to me at La Guardia Airport, from the looks of him, I figured he was dying. I alerted the flight attendants about the situation and after a harrowing flight we arrived at the airport in Fort Lauderdale. From there, Uncle Jim was transported to a hospital where I was told that he had suffered a cerebral hemorrhage several days before and that he most probably wouldn't recover.

UNCLE JIM WAS STILL a tough guy and a little brain bleed was not enough to finish him off. After several days, he was transferred to a worn out nursing home near the hospital, where he was scheduled to stay for a week or so. Uncle Jim had a private room. The help seemed conscientious, and he was being pampered as much as possible under the circumstances.

Joe, Kevin, Isabel, and I drove daily from Miami. Dino Celini's widow, Helena, brought homemade Italian Wedding Soup every few days. Auntie Doe's grandsons, Jimmy and Ricky, flew in from Las Vegas.

The first day Uncle Jim was at the recovery facility, a nurse walked into the room and said, "I want to interview you."

"Are you a reporter? It don't pay to get sick today. The problem is Medicare. They rob you and they don't even use a gun."

When she told him he was going to have to pee in a receptacle, he said, "I can go in a field. I can go in the grass. I cannot go in a bottle."

A few days into his stay, an elderly black man knocked shyly and entered Uncle Jim's room. "Mr. Alo," he said, "I saw your name on the door and I just had to come in and say 'hello.' My name is Phil. I worked with your gardener, David. And I wanted to come in and shake your hand because I happen to know you paid for David's funeral."

Uncle Jim chuckled and offered his gnarled hand. "Oh, yeah? Well, waddya you know about that," he said softly, gazing up at the man standing by his bedside.

IN A WEEK, Uncle Jim was stable enough to return to his apartment. The Sea Air Towers was filled with caregivers, and Tommy had lined up a couple of them through the management.

The day person turned out to be a blonde floozy who thought it was okay to apply toenail polish with her foot propped up on Uncle Jim's bed. The night person, an older and more qualified woman, did nothing but complain about the floozy.

The apartment was turned into a convalescent home, with a hospital bed set up in the living room. My uncle's beautifully tailored trousers were no longer practical, so I went out and bought him pull-on cotton pants. His expensive shoes were now obsolete, so I got him a pair of navy blue sneakers, certainly the first ones he had ever owned. He had plenty of nice Izod shirts and a fire-engine red cotton hat that he favored. The end result, with the sneakers, loose pants, and red hat, was that he looked like a very old child. From now on, he would be traveling by wheelchair, and as the weather cooled, he would still look presentable in his good sport jackets and the woolen scarves to protect him from getting the ever-fearsome *chill.*

I drove the forty-five minutes from my house to Hallandale every day. Sometimes, Joe would come with me and we would stop at Wolfie's, the old landmark delicatessen on Collins Avenue to bring potted chicken or matzah ball soup to Uncle Jim. On days that I couldn't come, I relied on Tommy, who was always around.

Uncle Jim had plenty of visitors. One day, I found a man (a producer from the West Coast) and two young women sitting in the living room. They were staring at Uncle Jim, who was no longer "with it." One of the women got up to stroll around and look at the photographs on the wall. Later, as they exited the apartment and walked up the hall, I heard her say, "Did you see the picture of Sinatra's parents? Why don't you ask him for that?" It was then that I realized my uncle needed protection from people who seemed more like scavengers than friends.

The hastily acquired help left a lot to be desired. Uncle Jim wanted to stay in his apartment, but I knew I couldn't keep the schedule up indefinitely. The last straw was when I got there to find that Tommy had Uncle Jim down by the pool in his wheelchair, surrounded by a group of men who hardly knew him, and had no business seeing him in his present condition. So-called "friends" that my uncle barely knew seemed to be popping up regularly. I was getting the feeling that Jimmy Blue Eyes was on display.

I knew what I had to do. Uncle Jim would have to come and live at my house. The hospital bed was transferred and we cleared out the small bedroom on the first floor. The room was just right to serve as my pint-sized uncle's sleeping quarters.

"This bed feels very good," he says, "I'm so tired." My uncle lies down on the hospital bed provided by Medicare. "Is this what I'm payin' five thousand *a* year for?" he asks.

I laugh, glad to see he still has his edge.

Every time he lies down, I wonder, will this be his last day? Or will he linger for a long time—no longer himself, but yet, pieces of himself? I try to fill in the missing pieces. I surround his bed with photos. Uncle Jim and Auntie Doe looking fabulous on their way to Hawaii in 1935. Myself, age twelve, with Jimmy Durante. Uncle Jim playing golf in the Fifties, his favorite photo. Uncle Jim with Mama and Papa Sinatra, looking every bit the gangster as he drags on a cigarette.

Most days, he sits in front of the TV and sleeps. I put the golf game on. Maybe in his sleep, he hears it and it comforts him. I want to put the pieces back together again. I feel like I'm losing parts of my life as my uncle is losing his.

It's strange to have Uncle Jim at our house. It feels like, suddenly and without notice, a lion moved in one day and took up residence in the den. If that happened—something so exotic—you wouldn't be able to take it all in, at first. You'd keep staring through a crack in the hallway door, trying to get used to things.

He's a toothless old lion now. Helpless, courageous, proud. I want to give him every shred of dignity possible.

"Just make me comfortable," he says. "I'm still the same Jimmy."

Today I left my uncle's apartment on Ocean Drive for the last time. The movers took away the furniture that came from the house on Monroe Street. All has gone to auction or been dispersed to whomever could use an armoire or a chair or a lamp.

I'm thinking now that my uncle no longer has any place at all. A person's home and their "things" are somehow all a part of who they are and have been. Our rustic home, with its terracotta floors and ceilings of planked Florida pine was somehow so wrong for Uncle Jim. Built in 1924 as a farmhouse in the middle of a mango grove, we had worked on it for years and loved its casual provincial charm. But, Uncle Jim belonged in a more cosmopolitan setting.

Once, a peacock landed on our roof and stayed there all day. Next day, it was gone. Like that peacock, Uncle Jim seems fundamentally out of place. Jimmy Blue Eyes doesn't belong in my home. It really doesn't suit him. But then, I know he's just "hangin' out a while," as he says. Until it's time to go.

When Uncle Jim first moved into my house, the older and wiser lady from Hallandale came along as his "day person." For the nighttime, I thought a man might be better because in the morning, he could help Uncle Jim bathe and it would be less embarrassing.

I hired a Jamaican gentleman named Tyrone, who turned out to be about as likeable as a Storm trooper. He insisted on a rigid schedule, which included giving my uncle a shower every morning at five a.m. Uncle Jim didn't want a shower at all, no less at 5 a.m. We began to cringe when we saw Tyrone walking up the driveway. After a week or so, we had had enough and I told him his services would no longer be required.

We went through a series of incompetents, until we found Kay. She became our "night person," a beautiful Haitian woman with a lilting accent and a gentle, caring heart. All of this was lost, however, on Uncle Jim, who thought Kay was a male prison guard. For the daytime, we found Nadine, also Haitian, a sweet young woman who had her nose in a book studying for a college degree every spare moment.

Kay had her hands full with Uncle Jim. He suffered from a form of dementia called Sundowner's Syndrome. Most often in the day, he was his old self. But as night approached and the hours went on, he lost all sense of time and place, saw shadows and people in the shadows, visited scenes of imagination and of the past.

Often, Kay would use her cell phone to call my bedroom in the middle of the night. I would put on my robe and come downstairs to sit with Uncle Jim. We had many fascinating conversations in the hours between dusk and dawn.

"You know, Carole, I never thought my favorite niece would be in this kind of business."

"What business is that, Uncle?"

"You know what I mean," he said slyly. "By the way, whose house is this?"

"It's my house."

"Well, how many houses do you own? I've never seen this one before."

"No?"

"No. And how can you afford a house like this, anyway?"

"I have a rich uncle."

Sometimes in the morning while eating breakfast, he would tell me about the night before. "I saw Meyer last night."

"You did? No kidding!"

"Yeah. He was sittin' right here on the couch."

"Well, it must have been good to see him."

"Yeah. It sure was."

"How'd he look?"

"A little thin."

Or:

"Your aunt was here last night."

"Oh, really?"

"Yeah. We got out of here and I took her to a football game. Say, you oughta fire that guard. He's no good. Where'd you get the help around here? They're from hunger."

Some days, Uncle Jim thought he was in the Bronx. "Say, I'd like to walk up the block and get a haircut and a shave."

"But Uncle," I'd say, or Nadine would say, or whoever was with him would say, because he was now Uncle Jimmy to everybody. "You can't walk to the barber shop, it's too far."

"Aw, what're you talkin' about? It's right up the street, by the zoo."

We were forced to accept the concept that Uncle Jim was living in "the Bronx!"

~

I BOUGHT Uncle Jim a green reclining wing chair, and we got a rolling table for his meals. Sitting on his chair in the den, he could see the pool through the French doors.

When I took him for an X-ray, the doctor said, "Mr. Alo, you have a scar and a shattered rib. Were you ever in the army?" Uncle Jim answered, "No, I got it in a heist."

The doctor said that Uncle Jim should try to walk every day. And he did. Two or three turns around the pool. At the end of the day, when Joe came home, Uncle Jim would say, "Joe, I did *nine* walks around the pool!"—and hold up various numbers of fingers to illustrate the lie.

One day, while doing his walks around the pool, Uncle Jim tried to escape over the wall. He sprinted through the cutting garden, trampling the flowers and knocking over a heavy sundial. Poor Nadine caught him and, panting and sweating, managed to get him back into the house. Then, she called Isabel.

Uncle Jim was sitting placidly on the den couch when Isabel arrived.

"Uncle Jimmy," Isabel began, "what were you trying to do?"

"I just wanted to go visit my pals."

"But Uncle, I think your pals are too far away."

"I think you're wrong, Isabel."

"Now Uncle, don't you trust me? I wouldn't lie to you. I think you're a little confused."

"Well, Isabel," said Uncle Jim, totally unflappable, "did it ever occur to you that it may be you who are confused?"

Uncle Jim often wore his woolen robe and scarf in the house because he claimed to be cold. At times, he shuffled into the dining room to eat with us and at times, he preferred to eat in the den while watching the news on television. He was still interested in politics and found President Clinton's troubles amusing.

"Politicians!" he said with disdain, "They produce nothin', they create nothin'. They live off the people."

His comments revealed his pragmatic point of view and his acceptance of the innate brutality of the human race. For instance, he had this to say about the 1991 beating of Rodney King:

> The blacks hate the Jews and the Jews hate everybody. Nobody rioted years ago, when thirteen Italians were lynched. Human beings hate each other. It's always been that way. You can't change human nature. We got worse beatin's than that. King is still alive. He's walkin' around, nothin's wrong with him. He got a beatin'. What's the big deal?

When clean cut, upstanding Kevin came over to spend some quality time with Uncle Jim he received invaluable nuggets of advice from his great-uncle:

"Remember. Keep your thoughts to yourself. Never let anyone know what you're thinkin'."

"Don't make enemies."

"Never make appointments in advance."

One day we asked him what he thought happened to Sam Giancana.

"Well, Christ! He went around all over the country sayin' that he put John Kennedy in the White House."

When we asked if he thought somebody wanted to shut Giancana up about that, he said:

"Does two and two make four? You figure it out."

WHERE'S THE MONEY?

Meyer Lansky was never far from Uncle Jim's thoughts. "I respected him more than anybody else I ever knew."

At dinner, one Sunday evening, Uncle Jim spoke about Meyer's wife, Teddy.

"She came to me and asked me to give her a few stories because she wrote a book and her publisher was askin' for the advance back. I told her, 'I can't give you any stories, Teddy. Everything Meyer and I did together was illegal.'"

"What was she gonna write about—what she cooked him for dinner?"

Then, he went on to talk about how little money Meyer left at the time of his death. Meyer's brother, Jake, was the "legitimate" partner, on paper—owner of Meyer's assets, such as shares in the Singapore Hotel and the Hawaiian Isle Motel. When Jake died six months after Meyer, his wife and daughters became the recipients of whatever Meyer had accumulated during his lifetime.

The stocks that Meyer left in trust to his family were practically worthless by the time his will was executed. He had often laughed about his shortcomings as an investor. As Uncle Jim said, "We owned all that beachfront property. We couldn't wait to give it away. That's how dopey we were."

In the end, Uncle Jim managed to round up additional money for Meyer's widow and his children, Sandy, Paul, and Buddy, by calling in various debts and obligations.

So where is the three hundred million that is so often attributed to Meyer Lansky? If that money really existed, why did his heirs get such a royal screwing? And if Meyer was such a "genius," then how is it that he didn't provide more carefully and abundantly for his loved ones? Another example of the chasm between reality and popular belief.

Several times a week, Tommy made the two-hour pilgrimage from his home in Palm Beach. I'd have Uncle Jim dressed, with money in his pocket, so that he could take Tommy out to lunch. Even though he was in a wheelchair, he still wanted to feel that he was in charge, and Tommy's presence helped to make him feel like 'the old Jimmy.'

Every month or so, Tommy would bring Uncle Jim's younger brother, Doctor Joe, the plastic surgeon, to visit. Through the years, I had barely seen him. Now he was aging and seemed a little befuddled. They looked very much alike, and I could see that there was a strong bond of brotherly love between them.

The widow Cellini came every week without fail. Helena was a petite ex-beauty queen who hailed from the South and had the proverbial Southern charm to prove it. She was genuinely fond of

Uncle Jim, who had been a friend and business partner to her husband, Dino, going back to the Havana days. She wasn't really my cup of tea and I think she felt the same about me—but she showed a lot of loyalty to my uncle so I welcomed her into my home.

I HAD BEEN URGING Uncle Jim to give *someone* power-of-attorney. Shortly before his stroke, Uncle Jim told me he was making Frankie Jr. the personal representative of his estate and giving him power-of-attorney. I felt that he was more comfortable with a man having those responsibilities. Being completely ignorant of such things, it didn't mean much to me, at the time. What it meant, after the stroke, was that Frankie was in charge of paying all the bills from Uncle Jim's bank account. That was all right with me, because I had my hands full just taking care of my uncle's day to day care.

There began to be signs of strain when Frankie warned me to keep a strict record of the spending that was coming out of Uncle Jim's cash. It clearly galled him that I was in possession of the $10,000 that my uncle had in his pocket on the day he went into the hospital, and he was letting me know that I'd better not be dipping into it for myself. I already knew that Frankie and his wife, Joy, were not friendly toward me, based on remarks that had been made to both my daughter-in-law and my friend, Loria. And I had to hide the feelings I had about the way they dumped my uncle onto the plane in order to extricate themselves from having to deal with a sick old man. During their occasional visits, I tried to maintain cordiality because I knew that we had to work together in caring for Uncle Jim and it was best to keep any bad feelings under wraps.

The nights were rough. Uncle Jim would roam through the house, trailed by Kay. One night, he went berserk and trashed his room, knocking over the television set and pulling pictures from the walls. I would call Frankie at three o'clock in the morning as I sat with Uncle Jim. Sometimes I did it because I was overwhelmed, and sometimes I did it out of spite, because I wanted him to know what we were going through. I would put Uncle Jim on the phone and let Frankie take a shot at calming him down.

One of the hardest aspects of my uncle's illness was the loss of his privacy and dignity. He insisted on going into the bathroom alone and I respected that. On the other hand, I was afraid he might fall, which he actually did once or twice. On those occasions when I was alone in the house with my uncle, I felt it necessary to peek through a crack in the bathroom door, to make sure he was safe. There was a chair in the bathroom and sometimes he would sit there, absently playing with the string on his pajamas. Sometimes, he would count his money. I made sure he always had cash in his pocket. He accused Nadine and Kay of stealing his money. Later, we would find the spots where he had hidden it. He seemed to feel safe in the bathroom, so we let him be.

In spite of these episodes, Uncle Jim was himself—a serene version of himself—a lot of the time. He still had the ability to charm. Medicare sent a woman who came once a month to check on him. She was an attractive African-American lady who always dressed in white and wore a turban, which I took to mean she was in a religious sect. She was quite a charmer herself, and she and my uncle hit it off very well.

"I'm of a curious nature," he told her. "I wanted to *learn*, not to make money. You know, just to satisfy myself."

Sometimes he made statements that left her puzzled. "It was all illegal. So what?"

Uncle Jim would ramble on while the woman listened intently, as if she knew what he was talking about. "I'm supposed to be an important guy—but I still say 'hello' to the bootblack."

"Silvana Mangano wrote me letters in the can. What a nice woman. Tony Quinn is also a hell of a nice guy. We had dinner at his house, a farmhouse outside of Rome. We spent many evenings there with him and his wife."

"You know," he told the woman, "I think my trouble is too much red sauce."

SIDNEY STROMBERG CALLED REGULARLY from the nursing home in Westchester where he was being treated for diabetes. Uncle Jim had tried, in vain, to convince him to control his weight. Now, he was in bad shape. Two loyal "dese-dems-and-dose" pals from the Bronx named Slim and Dickey called Uncle Jim religiously every week to keep his spirits up. They sounded like a couple of fun guys. It was them who called to give us the heartbreaking news that our dear Sidney—that connoisseur of Shakespeare who spent eighteen years of his life behind bars—had passed away.

Once, while Tommy was visiting, Uncle Jim fell asleep. Over a cup of coffee, Tommy began referring to a woman named Kris. I put on my best poker face and pretended that I knew what he was talking about. I had known there was a woman, through the years, but I had never heard a name. Now, I was hearing that, right up to the end, Kris had been in my uncle's life. As a woman, I was outraged at this betrayal of my aunt.

I thought about a recent conversation with my uncle.

"You know," he said," Now that your aunt is gone, I notice somethin'. I look at these other women and I see they're just pale in comparison. I mean, your aunt had *somethin'*. I don't know what it was. You can't forget her. She once sent me a card," he went on, placidly, "It said, 'You made all my dreams come true.'"

How can you explain the complexities of the human heart?

IN DECEMBER, Frankie Jr. and I discussed the fact that Uncle Jim was never going back to the New York apartment and there was no use in continuing to pay rent there. Uncle Jim had always been open about the contents of his will and I had a copy. He wanted me to have all of my aunt's things. I wanted many of the things that were meaningful to me, but I couldn't possibly keep everything.

When Frankie told me to go to New York and close the apartment, it caused a dilemma, because, technically, the furniture and other objects weren't mine until my uncle passed away. Frankie told me not to worry, just to send whatever I couldn't use to auction. There was also the question of a large breakfront that Uncle Jim was bequeathing to his step-daughter-in-law, in Las Vegas. I reminded Frankie that the breakfront needed to be shipped to her.

He corrected me. "That thing isn't goin' anywhere."

"Uh, Frankie, Uncle Jim has promised it to her. It's in the will."

"Well, I don't give a shit what he promised, she ain't gettin' it."

That was a big, red flag.

Isabel came with me to New York. The doormen all wanted to know how Uncle Jim was doing and sent their warm regards. The landlady, who lived on the second floor, was only concerned that I was going to try to take over the apartment. This was a possibility because I was a family member and had lived with them when they moved in, back in 1955.

A letter was slipped under the door informing me that I had to vacate immediately. We ignored the letter and continued on with the business of deciding what was to be shipped to Florida and what was going to auction. It was a lot of work and it was emotional.

In a few days, Isabel flew home and my friend, Geri, arrived to help me.

I'M up at 8 a.m. The auction people will be here in an hour and I'm feeling sick to my stomach. Letting go of my aunt's things is like sending a group of children off to the orphanage. My aunt's spirit is in each and every object.

A snooty young man comes from an Upper East Side shop to take a look at the old books. He tells me they're worthless, so I decide I'll take some with me. The sooty curtains, I'll throw away.

An antique dealer shows up. An elegant older man. He buys things, and then stays for a long time just to sit and talk. I'm talking about my childhood—my family. He says, again and again, "How wonderful to have people fighting over you! Two sets of parents, instead of one." He stays for quite a while, listening. A lovely man.

When the work was done and it was time to go, I went through the apartment for one last look. How empty and surreal it was, stripped of its guts. I walked out into the hall and took the elevator down to the lobby. I had to force myself to keep going. Out on the street, I hailed a cab. We pulled away from 19 West Fifty-Fifth, and I didn't allow myself to look back.

New York has never been the same for me since that day.

THE TRUCK ARRIVED in Miami with my aunt's things—now mine—and I began to distribute them throughout the house. These things were a part of my aunt, my uncle, and of the past that I could still keep close to me.

With Uncle Jim, everything went on as usual. He seemed illuminated from within. He had a stillness of spirit, as if everything superfluous had been burned away.

He continued to reminisce and as we listened, the picture of the life he had led and the rocky course he had navigated came into full focus. "Well, now you know the whole story," he would say. "That's how everything began. I know. I was there. They say I'm the last one."

Uncle Jim found comfort in the company of my son, Kevin, who would come over to give his great-uncle a shave or rub his shoulders. He told Kevin, "I don't regret anything. I've had good friends, a good life. I know I'm on my way out—but it's been a hell of a ride. I want my grandchildren and great-grandchildren to know that I wasn't the kinda guy they make me out to be. I'd like them to know how it all happened."

THE HOME STRETCH

Christmas 2000, but my uncle doesn't care. He's ninety-six and he's seen too many Christmases.

He tells me he wants to get it over with. But still he hangs on, his strong mind in steady decline since the hemorrhage that ravaged his brain. His indefatigable personality hangs in shreds now. His fierce independence is gone. I have all but stopped looking for the shards of light that signaled the temporary return of the man I knew. Occasionally, a smile or a shrug reminds me of the way he used to be.

I'm called downstairs and spend two-and-a-half hours with him in the middle of the night. He tells me that the nurses are "wrestlers." They are tossing him around "like a sack of potatoes."

"I'm in the hands of the Philistines," he says. "I'm a sick pup. I hope your feelings won't be hurt, but I have to leave. I don't get along well with your staff. They're manhandling me."

"Okay," I tell him. "But it's the middle of the night. Why don't you wait till tomorrow to leave?"

I get out the big albums and we look at photos from the Twenties. Some, even earlier than that. The pictures from the clubs . . . my uncle's million dollar smile . . . my aunt in the Forties, looking like a movie star . . . the Fifties, they're middle-aged now . . . dozens of pictures of them playing golf . . . the Sixties and Las Vegas . . . the Seventies, traveling through Europe . . . the Eighties, Auntie Doe looking old now, Uncle Jim seeming never to change.

Finally, I go upstairs to bed. I lie there thinking of the time when I won't be able to take this anymore. Then, what will I do? Where will he go? Wherever it is, how will they know how to take care of him the way I do? I think of all the little details . . . all his special needs and preferences. I think about how I know who he is and the way he's used to living.

Don't help him too much, he's very independent. Don't baby him, he'll resent that. Don't go into the bathroom with him, he's modest. Don't invade his privacy in any unnecessary way. Call him "Uncle Jim," he likes that. Cut his food into bite-sized pieces and watch that he doesn't choke.

Put in his hearing aids—take them out. He likes his scarf when it's the least bit cold. He can't sleep lying flat. He needs to spit a lot, so keep a stash of napkins handy. Look at the papers every morning and talk about the day's events, especially politics. You know, that's where Organized Crime is—in Washington.

Oh, my God. Only I would know a million little details. How can strangers understand the significance of it all? How can they understand who he is? Was? Who will care?

Uncle Jim inhabits my den by day. In the early evening, he announces he's ready for bed. I remove his shoes, carefully putting his cane aside, his "third leg," as he calls it. I cover him with the three or four blankets it takes to keep him feeling warm, remove his glasses, kiss him goodnight. Not long after that, he takes off on a journey and I hear his voice from the next room where I sit, watching TV.

"Yeah, those guys came from Chicago. They wined and dined 'em. I told them, I didn't want any part of that nickel & dime operation. Sure. A bottle cost ten or fifteen bucks and they charged them twenty. Well, I didn't want any part a' that half-baked deal. Sure, Julian Kaufman brought them in from Chicago. I knew 'em all."

I walk into the darkened room and touch his shoulder. "Uncle Jim, is everything all right?" He hardly acknowledges me and continues talking to the wall.

"Julian Kaufman was my partner. But I told them I don't want any part of that stuff. Just leave me out of it. What's that you say? Sure. I knew 'em all."

I know that Uncle Jim has traveled back in time to a world that existed some sixty or seventy years ago. A time that we can only imagine; a world that has become the stuff of legend. It's all there in his head and he relives it each night, the characters, long dead, returning to the stage. Upon the magic carpet of his mind, he calls them forth.

"I was with Meyer," he tells me. Or, "I was with your aunt. I don't know where she went. She was kidnapped. *These people* know what happened, but they won't tell me. She was here one minute and gone the next."

THE STRAIN WAS TAKING its toll. After seven months of caring for Uncle Jim in our home through all his ups and downs, the nighttime horrors, the falling, the thinking he was in the Bronx—going through eight different home caregivers, the loss of our privacy, and having no idea how long this might go on, we began thinking about an alternative.

I looked at a couple of nursing homes, focusing on dementia units. I was horrified by the regimentation and the zombies I saw lined up against the wall in their wheelchairs. That was not for Uncle Jim. A friend suggested a small, private assisted living facility that she knew of. Taking Isabel with me, I went to check it out. It was a private home that housed only nine or ten patients. It seemed like a comfortable place with pleasant surroundings. It was near my house and I thought it might give us the relief we were longing for.

Then, on a Sunday afternoon, I noticed a downturn in Uncle Jim's condition. He had choked on the fortified drink he liked so much and the liquid seemed to be gurgling around in his lungs. I called the paramedics and they thought he needed to be hospitalized. It turned out that he had pneumonia and had suffered another cerebral hemorrhage. I was advised to contact hospice care, which I did. When my uncle's brother, Dr. Joe, heard that, he was furious. He seemed to be under the impression that bringing hospice onboard meant we were just going to put Uncle Jim out on the ice and let the polar bears take care of it. After the hospice doctor explained things to him, he seemed to calm down. Uncle Jim was in the hospital for six days. On the seventh day, I had him transferred to the ALF, which hospice had looked into and approved.

We decided to give the Tender Loving Care Assisted Living Facility a try. I started out by furnishing my uncle's bedroom with familiar objects. Nadine stayed with him by day and Kay was there at night. I brought favorite foods and joined the small group of patients for dinner. Some of them were silent, but others were quite with it. One evening, an elegant old lady seated at the head of the dining table gazed inquisitively at Uncle Jim, who was busy concentrating on his soup. "Tell me, Mr. Alo, what did you do in your professional life? Were you a politician?"

"No," said Uncle Jim without missing a beat. "I wouldn't stoop that low."

Within a few days, I knew I had made a mistake. As well-meaning as the owner of the ALF seemed to be, they had their rules and didn't intend to bend them. One problem was the issue of showers. They insisted upon a daily shower that took place in the early morning hours. Uncle Jim, with his paper-thin skin, resented being "manhandled" and considered this a form of torture.

Four days after Uncle Jim moved to the ALF, Kay received a phone call while he was in the shower. She left him with someone on staff who allowed him to fall. He suffered a few bruises and lost an inch of skin on his arm. What was I thinking? I knew then that I would bring him home.

In the meantime, behind the scenes, a plot was afoot. Even before Uncle Jim was hospitalized, there were several conversations with Tommy about an idea he had hatched to take Uncle Jim back to the Sea Air Towers and re-install him in an apartment there. When I moved my uncle from the hospital into the ALF, the plot thickened. According to Tommy, what Uncle Jim needed was more of a *social life.* He seemed to have no concept of how fragile my uncle was, or the level of constant care and attention he required.

I told Tommy that I was bringing my uncle back to my house. He condescendingly informed me that it was up to *Dr. Joe* to make the decisions. This was news to me, since I was my uncle's designated health care surrogate. It was the first I had heard that there was anyone out there who thought my uncle's doddering eighty-eight-year-old brother had some sort of authority. Tommy told me that I should treat Dr. Joe with respect, to which I responded that I intended to treat him with respect, but that he was not in charge of Uncle Jim's care.

When Tommy first started talking about bringing Uncle Jim back to the Sea Air Towers and rehiring the same bimbo he had brought in before, I dismissed it as the wishful thinking of someone who really *wasn't* thinking. I realized that Tommy wanted better and more complete access to my uncle. What I didn't understand was how serious he was and that he would try to manipulate Dr. Joe in order to gain control. I didn't see that he and the Johnny-come-lately nephew, Frankie, would team up in an attempt to wrestle my uncle away from us, his intimate family.

Uncle Jim was with the people who were closest to him and who were most able to make informed decisions. My son, Kevin, was the apple of his eye and he was extremely fond of Kevin's wife, Isabel. He was comfortable with my husband, Joe. I was the child he had raised. To us, he was a man not a myth. Now, as death approached, he needed to be with what was real and what was loving, not with people who wanted to make themselves fare better through his presence.

Nadine received a call from Frankie asking her if she would like to care for Uncle Jim in an apartment in Hollywood. Next, he called the home care agency and told them of his plans to move my uncle. The director of the agency called me immediately. She said that she told him they didn't service Broward County and that she dealt with me, his designated caregiver. She said Frankie went ballistic.

Now I knew that Frankie and Tommy were going to try to take Uncle Jim away. In my mind, neither of these two were rocket scientists. And as for Dr. Joe, yes, he was my uncle's beloved brother, but he was a dithering Elmer Fudd who could barely take care of himself. None of these three was capable of caring for my uncle for whom, I knew, the clock was ticking down.

Frankie called and said, "Listen, Carole, I think what we'll do is, we'll put Unca' Jimmy back up in Hallandale where he can have more of a social life."

"Frankie," I said, "I don't think you get the picture. You haven't seen Uncle Jim in a few months. He's very frail and I think the end is near. We have hospice care and I'm bringing him back to my house.

"No, Carole, no, you're not. I'm coming down there and I'm gonna get him."

"I don't think so," I said, and hung up.

An hour later, we received a near-hysterical phone call from Frankie during which he issued orders that I was not to take my uncle out of the ALF and that he was being moved to the Sea Air Towers. I was so infuriated that I threw the phone to the floor. When Joe picked it up, Frankie was screaming, "I forbid you to go there and get Unca Jimmy." In an effort to mollify the situation, Joe said, "Listen, Frankie, do you really want Jimmy to be paraded around in his condition and seen by God knows who?"

"Yes," he screeched. "That's what I want!"

Early the next morning, I called my attorney, the venerable Monroe Dixon. He told me to get right over there and bring my uncle home. He also advised me to file for guardianship and said he would draw up the papers. I called Nadine and told her to have Uncle Jim ready to go.

I called the owner of the ALF and told her I was coming to get my uncle. I figured Frankie had contacted her and I didn't know if anybody was going to try to stop me, so I was plenty nervous on the drive over. When I got there, I said, "Uncle, I'm breaking you out of here."

"Good," he said. "They're like the Gestapo in this joint." He explained to me that the place had been built to house drunks. For a minute, I didn't get it. Then I realized that, in his mind, he had been languishing in some long gone institution—and he was happy to escape from the fantasies of incarceration that haunted him.

I got my uncle into the car as fast as I could and hauled ass out of there, feeling like a fugitive from an action movie. The thought of those Three Stooges trying to snatch my uncle away made my blood boil. I could have knocked all of their heads together.

My uncle and aunt extracted me—albeit with the participation of my parents—from my place in the natural order of things, and in doing so created a tangled web that took me a lifetime to unravel. Now, after all of that, these people thought they were going to shove me aside as if I didn't matter because I wasn't "blood?" No. Not possible. Uncle Jim was more of a father to me than my own father, and, I was the daughter *he chose.*

"I'm bringing you home, Uncle," I said as we sped through the streets on that sun-dappled morning.

"Alright, honey," was all he said. It would be his last ride.

That evening as we were finishing dinner, I asked Uncle Jim if he was happy to be back at my house.

"Yes, I am," he said, his voice like sandpaper, "but I'd like a change of scenery once in a while."

"Well, where would you like to go for the change of scenery?" I asked.

"I'd like to go to Frankie's house for a while, then I could come back here."

"Would you like to tell that to Frankie?"

"Yes, I would."

I dialed the number and Frankie answered. "Hi, Frankie, I have Uncle Jim sitting here and he'd like to speak to you."

Knowing full well that Frankie and his wife would not want the responsibility of taking care of Uncle Jim, I handed the phone to my uncle and listened as he repeated what he had just told me. I'm happily imagining the two-step Frankie is having to do on the other end of the line.

"I can't hear you," Uncle Jim says, trying to adjust the hearing aid that never worked. "Talk to Carole."

I took the phone and seized the moment to attempt a cease-fire on behalf of my uncle. Swallowing my true feelings, I said "Listen, Frankie, why don't we try to set our differences aside for the sake of Uncle Jim's best interest?" Frankie said that he would be down in a week to see Uncle Jim and we would resolve the situation then.

A week can make a vast difference in the life of a person of ninety-six. When Frankie and Joy arrived at my house, they understood immediately that the reports they had been receiving from Tommy about Uncle Jim's glowing health had been ridiculous. They could see that, rather than being "in need of more company"— he was on his deathbed.

Later that day, Frankie met with Tommy and Dr. Joe. He told them that Uncle Jim wasn't going anywhere. And that was that.

Tommy had been the architect of the whole sequence of events surrounding the last few weeks of my uncle's life. He was desperate to get Uncle Jim back to the Sea Air Towers. After all, he was the sidekick of Jimmy Blue Eyes. The one who maintained Uncle Jim's identity in the world. "You're a legend, Jim," he would say.

It was good for my uncle to have had Tommy around in his final years. Tommy was the last in a long line of gofers and yes-men. He had done all the little everyday things for Uncle Jim and massaged his ego as well. I understood all of that. But it never occurred to me that Tommy would try to use Dr. Joe and Frankie in order to wrench control of my uncle away from me in his final days.

Tommy was now persona non-grata—and good riddance.

GOODBYE TO THE OLD LION

In the last days of his life, "Just make me comfortable," became Uncle Jim's mantra. He knew what was happening and he endured it with the dignity of a king.

"I'm still the same Jimmy," he repeated. Despite his enfeebled body, he was teaching us courage—letting us know that the spirit remains unchanged.

He stopped eating. He stopped coming into the den and remained in his bed. Sweet Nadine kept vigil beside him in the tiny room. "You have to accept Jesus," she pleaded with him.

"No, honey, I don't believe in that."

"Auntie Doe believed in God," I offered.

"Well," he said, "that's her prerogative."

Nadine refused to give up. "Uncle Jimmy, would you *mind* if I read to you from the Bible?"

He said that would be all right and so, for several days, she did. One day, she asked him again if he would accept Jesus into his heart and this time he said, simply, "Okay."

In that last week, there appeared a brief window of time when he acquired clarity. We had this conversation about the whole progression of how I came to live with them. How I should forgive my mother and no one was to blame. He said that I was the one who was really hurt by it all. I told him that I've had a great life and wouldn't have had it any other way.

Later that same day, his voice was a rasp and a whisper but his eyes burned with a bright light as he remembered:

> A couple of years ago, I was up in the Bronx and I ran into an old-timer who reminded me of a fight I was in over seventy-five years ago. It happened at a spot called Quarry Road. My opponent was also Jimmy—Jimmy DeLeo—I still remember his name. We both stripped to the waist and proceeded to go at it. You know—with our fists. That was the way you settled disputes in those days. There was quite a mob around us. Then the cops showed up and we all ran like hell. Can you imagine this guy rememberin' that fight? Seventy-five years ago!

This would be Uncle Jim's last story. The following day he turned his face to the wall and refused even water.

In spite of everything, he had always been able to access his old ability to enjoy life. But during his last few months, it was difficult for that huge life force to be trapped in a body that was losing the ability to contain it. "Jesus Christ," he would say, "how long am I gonna feel this way?" It never occurred to him that he was ninety-six and it wasn't going to get any better.

On a Friday evening, Kevin came over and cooked fish. After that, he sat at Uncle Jim's bedside for a while—talking to him and telling him how much we all loved him—how much he meant to us. He also threw in a few remarks about Clinton and Bush, trying to get a rise out of Uncle Jim, the way you always could by mentioning a politician or two.

At seven o'clock, Joe and I went up to our bedroom. A few minutes later, the phone rang. It was Kay calling from downstairs. "Miss Carole, come down quick!"

Joe rushed down and I lingered behind. When I found the courage to go downstairs, I went and stood by his bed, staring down at the wizened figure that occupied so little space. Kay, shaken, had withdrawn to another part of the house along with Joe and Kevin and Isabel. All were weeping.

I sat down by my uncle's bed and gazed at his face, drinking it in. He was an old lion. *I feel like I'm five years old inside and I don't want you to go. Are you going to leave me behind?*

I felt like there was a cord attaching us to each other—even imagined that maybe now I would cease to exist.

ON THE DAY when he turned his face to the wall, just before that physical gesture that spoke volumes, he said his last words, to nobody in particular.

"On Sunday," he said, "let's have a picnic. We'll bring sandwiches and beer."

He was back in the Bronx at last. He was wearing a straw hat and he was young. Very young.

CAROLE CORTLAND RUSSO

IF I'M quiet and I listen well, I can still hear his voice and feel the strength of his character.

> Whatever I did, I always did it like Jimmy. I always tried to have integrity. No matter what I did as I went through life, I never changed. Whether I was fourteen or forty—I was always Jimmy. I'm still the same Jimmy. Read that poem *IF* by Rudyard Kipling. That says it all. If you can live by that, you'll be all right.

EPILOGUE

A wake was held in Florida. I displayed pictures of my uncle at all stages of his life. Tommy was there, and Doctor Joe, but they kept their distance. Kay and Nadine, my two Haitian angels showed up decked out in their best finery—Kay all in black and Nadine in white. Their beauty struck me.

So many people came to pay their respects. Near the end of the day, a woman approached me. She was petite, blonde, and well preserved. "We lost a good friend, didn't we?" was all she said.

"Yes, we did," I answered. With that, she turned and walked away. I knew, at once, that she was the other woman. Kris.

IN NEW YORK, the funeral was handled by Frankie Jr. Instead of having Uncle Jim at Campbell's in Manhattan, where everyone else in the family had been, he chose to use a local funeral home in the Bronx. The old neighborhood. Maybe it was fitting.

There was a Mass at Our Lady of Mt. Carmel. I don't think Uncle Jim would have cared for it, but what difference did it make? At Woodlawn Cemetery my uncle and aunt were finally and eternally reunited. Jimmy and Flo. Like Ham and Eggs.

All my life, I accepted without question the reality in which I found myself. Sleep-out Louie and Killer Kane. Potatoes Kaufman, Bugsy Siegel, Cockeye Johnny Dunn, Banjo, Jimmy Blue Eyes. What an array of characters. What a party. What a circus.

I've thought a lot about my family. None of them should have been cast as parents. However, I loved them and learned from them. My mother taught me about loss and betrayal—a sense of the tragic. From my father I learned compassion because I came to understand that he knew not what he did. From my aunt I learned to have a vision for myself—a belief in the irrefutability of destiny.

As for Uncle Jim, I'll have to be content with the unresolved riddle of his life. From him, I learned about duality—that nothing is what it seems.

"IF"

~RUDYARD KIPLING

If you can keep your head when all about you
    Are losing theirs and blaming it on you,
If you can trust yourself when all men doubt you,
    But make allowance for their doubting too;
If you can wait and not be tired by waiting,
    Or being lied about, don't deal in lies,
Or being hated, don't give way to hating,
    And yet don't look too good, nor talk too wise:

If you can dream—and not make dreams your master;
    If you can think—and not make thoughts your aim;
If you can meet with Triumph and Disaster
    And treat those two imposters just the same;
If you can bear to hear the truth you've spoken
    Twisted by knaves to make a trap for fools,
Or watch the things you gave your life to, broken,
    And stoop and build 'em up with worn-out tools:

If you can make one heap of all your winnings

"IF"

And risk it on one turn of pitch-and-toss,
And lose, and start again at your beginnings
And never breathe a word about your loss;
If you can force your heart and nerve and sinew
To serve your turn long after they are gone,
And so hold on when there is nothing in you
Except the Will which says to them: 'Hold on!'

If you can talk with crowds and keep your virtue,
Or walk with Kings—nor lose the common touch,
If neither foes nor loving friends can hurt you,
If all men count with you, but none too much;
If you can fill the unforgiving minute
With sixty seconds' worth of distance run,
Yours is the Earth and everything that's in it,
And—which is more—you'll be a Man, my son!

ACKNOWLEDGMENTS

I had been writing about my uncle, Vincent "Jimmy Blue Eyes" Alo and our family for a couple of years when I got a call from an old friend, Barbara O'Daly, asking me to join a Memoir class. I jumped at the chance, bolstered by the belief that I would be sitting in the back row, taking notes. Had I known that the Professor was going to treat me like the other fifteen writers (post-grads and teachers), I'm sure I would have declined.

But, there I sat while fifteen writers talked about my pages as if I was in another room, or in my case, another universe. *Oh, the horror!* To them, my subject matter was verboten!

Mention the word *gangster* and you let loose something that takes on a life of its own. After all, they had seen movies, television shows, and documentaries about the *mob*. They knew everything there is to know! No matter that I was raised by a *gangster* and grew up around the *mob*; they knew the territory better.

Fifteen intelligent writers pelted me with pithy questions and statements. I was struck by the depth of their prejudice. No matter how hard I tried, I couldn't break their preconceptions of what my uncle, the mobster, must be like. "Weren't you afraid of him?" One asked. I answered, in all seriousness, "No, it's more likely that he was afraid of me." That left them stunned.

And so, my first acknowledgement is to those writers for giving me a peek at the uphill battle I was facing and to Dr. Kitty Oliver for enlightening me about the rules of the craft.

Big, big thanks to my publisher, Stephanie Larkin of Red Penguin Press, for bringing this book to life. I give a huge thanks to Erin Brown, my editor, who gave such great feedback. Special thanks to Dr. Stacy Davids, who generously shared her writing expertise and to Eric Dezenhall who believed I had a story to tell.

What would I do without my extraordinary friends? Loria Parker, who shared my history, Julie Morgan, who always had my back, Ann Crumb, my brilliant Acting buddy, and, my beloved sidekick, Geri Frank. You are truly my sisters.

I must remember Robbie Buckley-Burns, no longer with us, who guided me for years with her unconditional love and pure genius.

And, a special thanks to Norma Davids. Without her invaluable assistance, this book simply would not have been written.

Lastly, love and thanks to my wonderful family!

ABOUT THE AUTHOR

CAROLE CORTLAND RUSSO is an actress/singer whose featured roles in film, television and theatre have won her much acclaim. Among her many stage roles was *Eva Peron* in EVITA, *Mama Rose* in GYPSY and Aldonza in MAN OF LA MANCHA.

She won a Carbonnel Award Nomination from the South Florida Critics for *Mother* in A NEW BRAIN and *The Countess* in A LITTLE NIGHT MUSIC. In New York, she was lauded by Cabaret Critics and developed a reputation as a Singer's singer.

Carole was raised by her Uncle, Vincent "Jimmy Blue Eyes" Alo ~ one of the most significant crime figures of the twentieth century and a giant among Mafiosi. His life was filled with wise guys, celebrities and crooked politicians. Always a secretive man, in time, he began to talk. Carole took notes as he tallied up the score. "Was I a good guy or a bad guy?" Jimmy asked. "I'm an enigma, even to myself."

The soul of a gangster is a mystery Carole struggles with ~ even today. Being raised in the Damon Runyon world of her family has given her a rich story to tell. Most of all, she would like to set the record straight as she promised her Uncle she would.

Carole lives with her husband, Joe, in a 1924 Florida farmhouse with Sophia, the tortoiseshell cat and Sam, the world's smartest dog.